Looking at Wine Through a Different Window
by John Pulos

To see John Pulos in action, go to Wagner Vineyards' Virtual Tasting Series: https://Wag.Wine/VirtualSeries2020

John is featured in An Hour to Remember, Bordeaux in FLX and What a Bottle Says About Your Wine.

REVIEWS OF THE JOHN PULOS WINE-TASTING EXPERIENCE AT WAGNER VINEYARDS IN LODI, NY

Insightful, Fresh & Wholesome Experience Over Good Wine

Have you ever done a wine tasting but not understood the jargon...? Ever wish someone could help contextualize your experience by giving you some FUN insight into the wine, grapes, taste, aroma?...John Pulos gave us an in-depth look at the history of Seneca Lake, the jargon used for wine, the grapes, the region, and more. We left feeling much more connected and educated via laughs and drinks. On top of that, the property offers stunning views to the lake and plenty of outdoor seating. Thank you, John!

Awesome Wine-Tasting Experience

John is hilarious, smart and witty. He knows more about wine than anyone I have come across on the wine trail. He made us laugh and smile the entire time. I would come back just to chat with him again!

Fantastic!

What a great experience! We've been to many wineries in the Finger Lakes. This was our first trip to Wagner's and one of the best. Our tasting with John was fantastic, both the wines and the experience. They have some great dry reds and unique blends, but John was the absolute highlight of our experience. We got a great education on the history of grapes and winemaking while enjoying our tasting. He is a true gem. Will definitely be back. Came in for a taste, left with a case!

Incredible Experience

This was our first visit to Wagner Vineyards. We have been to NAPA and Sonoma, but we have never had a wine tasting experience like the one we had on Sunday. John P. started off testing our knowledge of wine a bit, and crafted a tasting approach that thankfully left some of the basics behind. It did not feel like a canned spiel, he did not tell us what flavors we would be tasting in the wine but rather an incredible history and "Family Tree" of grapes and growing climates...It was the best tasting experience we ever had. Wagner Vineyards is a "must" stop if you like wine and are the least bit interested in some of its history and the history of the area. The wines were the best we tasted in the region. Be sure to make a reservation at Wagner Vineyards and ask for John P. Everywhere else will pale in comparison.

John, the Gem!
The wines were wonderful! The gentleman pouring the wine made the experience extraordinary! John Pulos is a gem! He told us the history behind each wine. He also gave us a language lesson, translating many wine terms into English for us, making the experience even more enjoyable! Hang onto him tightly! He represents your brand well.

Can't Miss!
What an amazing tasting. John is a local legend and cannot be missed. Extensive knowledge of the Finger Lakes wine region as well as wine as a whole. Would highly suggest stopping here on a day of tastings.

A Rich History to Some Fabulous Wines
What a wonderful place to start our wine tasting journey. John took me under his wing and taught me...about the region, each type of wine, and the history behind it all. John is by far the most personable, knowledgeable, and upbeat man I've met in a while. He teaches in a captivating way and really knows how to pinpoint your preferences for wine. John describes the tastes of each selection, painting a culinary experience on your imaginative taste buds, pairing wine with suggestions for courses from start to finish of a meal. Wagner struck gold in the combination of their staff and their incredible wines. After this awesome experience, I can say with certainty that I will be visiting again! Thank you!

Dedication

I've always noticed that authors invariably dedicate their books to someone. Even though I never thought that I would write a book, I couldn't help wondering to whom I might dedicate a book if I ever actually got around to writing one. The answer was easy.

I dedicate this book to my daughter, my Morgane "Hobie Girl," who has always been my greatest achievement and my greatest joy.

Acknowledgements

I want to thank the Wagner family at Wagner Vineyards for providing the forum for me to put this book together. I am certain that, from the top of the tasting menu to the bottom, the wine I pour at Wagner's is the best wine in the Finger Lakes Region. My thanks to the Wagner family for always allowing me to *"do it my way."*

When the Covid-19 pandemic forced the winery to close to visitors from March through June 2020, the Wagners kept me on board and graciously allowed me to use my down time at the winery to work on this book. They have supported me through every step of this process. Thank you to John and Debbie, and Laura, and their children: Ginny, Steven, Kevin, and Ian.

Many thanks to Ann Raffetto, Winemaker Emeritus, who for 36 years created the award winning wines at Wagner Vineyards. Her technical advice in the creation of the appendices was invaluable.

I also need to thank my fellow staff members who make every day at Wagner Vineyards enjoyable. They look after me as if I am their favorite grandfather. I consider all of them to be my friends. To a great degree, I have been working on this book while they toiled at the *real* work at the winery. Thank you, Wayne and Wayne (yes, there are two Waynes), and Julia, Val, Victoria, Faith, Leah, Jennifer,

Kendra, Austin, Marjorie, Katie, Alex, Mike, Jess, and my daily donut man, "An-do."

I want to thank Elizabeth Peterman for the cover photo. It is exactly what I envisioned when the name for the book came to me.

I also want to acknowledge my editor, Donna Himelfarb. We became instant friends when we met in 2016. Since then, her children, Erica and Asher, and son-in-law, Jonny, have "adopted" me into their family. I'm delighted to be the unofficial grandfather of Erica and Jonny's son, Oliver, who was born in 2018. (Erica also contributed her eagle-eye proofreading skills to this manuscript.) Donna is a professional editor whose grasp of the English language is second to none. This book is only as good as I hope it is because of the hours she spent editing it. When she finished, I was excited to read it. Thank you Donna, I am forever grateful.

TABLE OF CONTENTS

Beef

Poultry

Pork & Lamb

Seafood

Pasta

Dessert

APPENDICES

INTRODUCTION

Who am I—and why am I writing a book about wine?

I have lived in the Finger Lakes region of Central New York for all of my nearly-73 years. I graduated from high school in 1966 and from Hobart & William Smith Colleges in 1970. I taught school from 1970 until 1985, when I took over the management of my family's restaurant in the Watkins Glen area.

During my 15-year teaching career, I coached wonderful young men in both basketball and football. The novel, "Heaven is a Playground," was published in 1976. It was written by Rick Telander of Sport's Illustrated and the Chicago Tribune. It is still listed as one of the Top 15 sports books ever written. The book is about the summer that the young Telander spent on the playgrounds of Brooklyn with many young men, some of whom were playground legends, and many of whom had played for me at Glen Springs Academy during my teaching and coaching days.

Until 1985, my alcoholic beverage of choice was gin. I quickly discovered that I could not show up at the restaurant at 5:30 a.m., surrounded by the aroma of eggs, bacon and sausage, with a gin hangover. That's when I switched to drinking wine.

My first wine of choice was German Liebfraumilch, which I soon found to be too sweet. That's when I began to sample wine from the handful of new wineries that were springing up around Seneca Lake, the largest of NY's Finger Lakes.

Our restaurant, Chef's Diner, was very popular. Along with responsibility for running the restaurant, my dad passed on to me the responsibility of serving on various tourism boards. In addition to chairing the Tourism Committee of the Schuyler County Chamber of Commerce, I was also asked to serve on the Board of Directors of the Finger Lakes Tourism Alliance. That board, based in Penn Yan, is the oldest continuously operating tourism organization in the United States. I was elected to the Board of Directors of the New York State Restaurant Association and served as the Chairman of the Southern Tier Chapter of the Restaurant Association. In addition, I served on the Hobart & William Smith Board of Trustees for 16 years.

As the number of wineries in the Finger Lakes grew and grew, and because I was a member of various tourism boards, I frequented the wineries regularly. I constantly heard from one tasting associate after another, "You will taste apples, pears, and apricots; you will find it full-bodied, with high acidity and lovely minerality."

"Minerality"?! When was the last time you ate a rock that you liked? Acid? Full Bodied? No two people seemed to have the same definition for "full bodied"! I could never taste any of the fruits that they told me that I should be tasting. I may have liked the wine, but couldn't help wondering if something was wrong with me because I could not taste an apple or a pear or an apricot. Even though I assumed that I would be in the restaurant business for the rest of my life, I told myself over 20 years ago, "If I ever pour wine for a living, I WILL DO IT DIFFERENTLY!"

My dad opened Chef's Diner in 1949. Fifty-seven years later, on a Wednesday in July 2006, he worked in the kitchen all day. The following morning, he woke up feeling ill, so I took him to the hospital. He was dead on Sunday.

Before he fell into a coma, my father said two things to me. "Take care of your mother, Son." (They married at age 19, right after Pearl Harbor. Their love story lasted 64 years.) And, "Sell that God damn place! Do not end up like me." He was 84 years old when he died. After working there for 22 years, I sold the restaurant in 2007 and started a small catering company, specializing in high end, five-course dinners for very small groups.

For one of my first dinners, I was asked to pair the five courses with five red wines. At that time I drank only dry white wine. Never willing to do anything halfway, I decided to take a job at a local winery to learn more about wine and, specifically, red wine.

What follows are my years of research leading me to pour wine without naming specific fruits, or mentioning "full-bodied" or "minerality." I pour wine by teaching and explaining its history, its DNA, and why it is popular. It is a unique approach to pouring and talking about wine.

I write this for people who know a great deal about wine, for those who sit with friends and can discuss and distinguish between a Riesling from the Mosel, a Riesling from the Alsace, or a Riesling from the Finger Lakes.

But this book is also written for those who simply enjoy wine but have no idea what the Mosel or the Alsace are.

I am mentioned throughout the book, "Heaven is a Playground." The author, Rick Telander, thanks me in the book's acknowledgments. (I even gave a copy to my parents that Christmas, with my autograph, and mentioning that our family was officially ensconced in the Library of Congress.) I now enter that great library again, with this, my first book. A book that will make you think that you are...

"LOOKING AT WINE THROUGH A DIFFERENT WINDOW!"

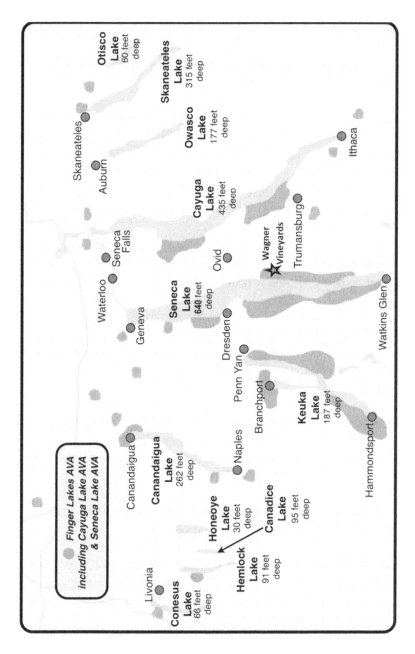

The Finger Lakes Region of Central New York

Chapter One: Noble Grapes and Wagner Vineyards

In August 2016, my wine journey led me to Wagner Vineyards, located on the east side of Seneca Lake in Lodi, New York. I had previously worked at Arcadian Estate Winery (now Barnstormer), Glenora Vineyards (the oldest winery on Seneca Lake), Finger Lakes Distillery (a 4-year respite from wine, where I learned about distilled products, most specifically, whiskey), finally landing at Wagner Vineyards.

While at the distillery, I researched the history of American whiskey (rye and bourbon). My time at Wagner Vineyards has led me to do the same, but with all things related to the creation and enjoyment of wine.

I have researched the history of our wines, our Noble Grapes. I share this history with our many customers, always eschewing the customary mentions of fruity taste, full-bodied character and, most especially, "minerality"!

The New York State Farm Winery Act of 1976 permitted anyone growing grapes to make wine in New York. Glenora Wine Cellars and its owner, Gene Pierce, began construction of their production and retail facilities in March 1977. The production area was ready for the 1977 harvest. (Bill Wagner actually lent a tank to Gene to help with that first harvest.) The Glenora tasting area opened in May 1978, making it the first of its kind on Seneca Lake.

Meanwhile, Bill Wagner wanted to fulfill *his* dream to open a facility unlike any other in the state. With his family and friends, he built the iconic octagon-shaped facility that remains to this day, more than 41 years later, unique in the Finger Lakes.

To understand the full history of wine in the Finger Lakes, you must understand the three types of grapes that are grown in the region.

European grapes grown on American soil are referred to by wine aficionados as Vitis Vinifera grapes.

These Vitis Vinifera grapes are the Noble Grapes that you will read about below. They are the Rieslings, the Chardonnays, the Cabernets, the Pinot Noirs and more.

Grapes that are native to American soil are called Vitis Labrusca. Many of these grapes were here when the first European settlers—or invaders, depending on how you look at it—got off the boats in the early 1600s. In the Finger Lakes Region, today's most popular indigenous grapes are Catawba, Concord, Delaware, Isabella, and Niagara.

When God created Europe, He gifted it with wonderful grapes: the Pinots, the Cabs, the Sauvignon Blancs, the Merlots and more. By the time God got around to North America, I suspect He was tired or just pissed off. Sure, we got grapes and, therefore, wine, but it tasted like grape juice. God also gave us corn and turkeys, but wine created from native grapes did not—and does not—enhance the taste of food.

The third category of grapes is referred to as "hybrid." Grapes, apples, cherries, etc., begin as flowers. A viticulturist is someone who studies and implements techniques related to growing grapevines in order to produce the grapes necessary for wine production. Viticulturists create new grapes by manually cross-pollenating the flowers of grapes in a laboratory setting. The popular Honey Crisp apple was created in a lab at the University of Minnesota and released in 1991. The popular white hybrid grape (and wine), Cayuga White, was developed by Cornell University and released to the Finger Lakes in 1972.

Italian explorer Giovanni da Verrazzano, who sailed under the flag of the King of France, was the first European to explore the Atlantic coast of North America, in search of a passage to the Pacific Ocean. In 1524, he sailed from Florida to New Brunswick in search of the non-existent Northwest Passage. He was the first European to sail into both the New York and Narragansett Bays. (It would be another 85 years before Henry Hudson would sail into New York Bay and up the river that bears his name.)

According to Thomas Pinney, author of "A History of Wine in America," Verrazzano wrote: "[There are] many vines, growing naturally, which growing up, tooke hold of the trees as they doe in Lombardie, which if by husbandmen they were dressed in good order, without all doubt they would yield excellent wines." These were "our" Vitis Labrusca grapes. (And, to set the record straight, they do *not* make "excellent" wines.)

After Hudson, the Dutch laid claim to the area now known as Manhattan. By 1647, Dutch colonists became the first to plant European Vinifera grapes. For reasons that were unknown at the time, these early vineyards of European grapes failed. When Thomas Jefferson left the presidency in 1809, he planted Chardonnay grapes at his Virginia plantation, Monticello. They, too, failed. It wasn't until the middle of the 19th Century that the culprit would be identified: the American phylloxera grape louse, which eats the roots of Vinifera grapes. **(See APPENDIX I)**

New York's famed Erie Canal, which connects Buffalo and Lake Erie to Albany and the Hudson River, was completed in 1825. The canal made it possible to ship agricultural and manufactured products to New York City and beyond. It was also in 1825 that the Reverend William Bostwick moved from Albany to Hammondsport, at the southern end of Keuka Lake in the Finger Lakes Region of New York. There, Bostwick established an Episcopal Church in Hammondsport.

Reverend Bostwick maintained a large garden while in Albany, where he experimented with native American grapes. In conversations with his new friends and members of his new congregation in Hannondsport, he talked of growing grapes and making his own wine for his church services. In 1829, a parishioner donated a large plot of land, where Bostwick planted Isabella and Catawba vines. A few years later, he introduced his own wine at his Sunday church services. It must have been pretty good, because the congregation's weekly attendance grew and grew. Taking advantage of his regular audience, he encouraged congregants to take vine cuttings from his garden to establish their own vineyards.

By the late 1840s, Finger Lakes grapes were being shipped to New York City. By 1870, Hammondsport was home to over 3,000 acres of vineyards. Vineyards were now planted on Seneca and Cayuga Lakes. By the turn of the century, the Finger Lakes boasted almost 15,000 acres of grapes. Grapes became a major industry and they were shipped to many East Coast markets.

Reverend Bostwick also asked the residents of this new grape-growing region to make wine. Cottage winemakers paved the way for the area's first winery in 1860. The Pleasant Valley Wine Company was established in Hammondsport. By 1862, it was shipping wine to New York City. Bonded "Number One," Pleasant Valley was the first bonded winery in America. (Without going into too much detail, wine "in bond" is wine that is stored before it is sold; a federal tax on the wine is paid by the seller.) Pleasant Valley used both Catawba and Isabella grapes.

Pleasant Valley was followed in 1865 by the Urbana Wine Company (later known as the Gold Seal Vineyards). Next was Walter Steven Taylor, who started a grape juice company in 1880; by 1882 he, too, was making wine. The history of these first three wineries in the Finger Lakes is deep and storied. It is a history that has been well-told, so I am not about to go into great detail, but will highlight some of the rich history that has led the Finger Lakes to its current status as the "Number One Wine Region in the United States" (USA Today, 2018 and 2019)

The three Hammondsport wineries flourished, sending their wines up and down the East Coast. Pleasant Valley brought in French-trained Champagne makers. By 1867, its sparkling wine had won an award in Europe. In 1873, Pleasant Valley's Great Western Champagne was awarded a gold medal in Vienna, and Hammondsport took its place on the world's wine map. Sadly, the great forward motion made by Hammondsport's "Big Three" ended abruptly in 1919, with the passage of the 18th Amendment to the United States Constitution, which you probably know as Prohibition.

The 18th amendment declared that, "After one year from the ratification of this article the manufacture, sale, or transportation of intoxicating liquors within, the importation thereof into, or the exportation thereof from the United States and all territory subject to the jurisdiction thereof for beverage purposes is hereby prohibited."

Though wine-making in Hammondsport ceased to exist in its former glory, Pleasant Valley, Gold Seal and Taylor Wine Company managed to survive Prohibition.

The wineries survived by making grape juice and wine for sacramental and "medicinal" purposes. Yes, wine was allowed in churches, and Americans seemed to pray with increased fervor as Sunday church services swelled with new worshippers!

Charles Walgreen opened his first food-front store in Chicago in 1901. By the time Prohibition took effect in 1920, his chain had grown to 20 stores. The stores dispensed prescriptions, thereby making them pharmacies. Alcohol (wine) was permitted, not only during church services, but, along with whiskey, was allowed by the Prohibition act for medicinal purposes and dispensed by pharmacies.

During this period of Prohibition, in 1922, Walgreens is credited with creating the malted milkshake. Take your kids to Walgreens and get them a milkshake while you wait for the pharmacists to dispense your whiskey and wine, for medicinal purposes only, of course. The formula seemed to work. By 1934, a year after Prohibition ended, Walgreens had expanded to 601 stores in 30 states.

Taylor Wine Company found another way to survive, selling kits that contained grape juice and yeast, as well as instructions on how to make wine. If you made your own wine (or whiskey) and did not sell it to anyone else, you were left alone.

After the end of Prohibition, the Big Three geared up to resume wine production on a larger scale. Many of the vineyards in the Finger Lakes had dried up because of little to no demand for their grapes. It takes 3 to 5 years to get usable fruit after planting a grape vine. When Prohibition ended, Gold Seal Vineyards brought the French Champagne maker, Charles Fournier, to the United States. With the success that Pleasant Valley had enjoyed with their Great Western Champagne, Gold Seal decided to re-energize itself with the production of sparkling wine. Fournier originally planned to stay in Hammondsport for only a year. Instead, he spent the rest of his life there, dying there in 1983.

Let's sidetrack for a minute and go to Odessa, Ukraine, where we find a young viticulturist named Konstantin Frank. In 1948, Frank was awarded a Doctorate from Odessa Polytechnic Institute. He had successfully planted Vitis Vinifera in the cold climate of Ukraine by grafting cold-weather rootstock to Riesling, Chardonnay, and Pinot Noir grapes. He came to America in 1951, and in 1953 he went to work for Cornell University. There, he applied the same grafting techniques to the Vitis Vinifera grapes in the cold climate of the Finger Lakes.

During this period, Charles Fournier brought Dr. Frank to Hammondsport. Together, they pioneered the planting of Vinifera grapes, by grafting to cold-weather root stock obtained from Canada. Frank opened his Vinifera Winery—known today as the Dr. Konstantin Frank Winery—in Hammondsport in 1962. These two men pioneered the growth of this region into a world class wine producing area. As previously mentioned, there is much more to this story.

Frank's doctorate was awarded three years after the end of World War II. The Allied attack to liberate Europe from the German War machine got underway on June 6, 1944. Known as D-Day, the first wave of soldiers to hit the beaches of France's Normandy coast experienced a casualty rate that was close to 90 percent. My dad, who was 22 years old at the time, survived the first wave to hit Omaha Beach. During the following week, 326,000 troops would enter France with the goal of reaching Berlin. Eleven months later, the war in Europe ended.

The returning soldiers who fought their way across France and Germany had tasted Vinifera wines, eventually returning stateside, where these wines were unavailable. (Cabernet Sauvignon had been planted in part of California in the 1880s, but most of it was lost during prohibition.) After the war, the US had a whole new generation of wine drinkers who demanded better wine.

Americans' demand for better wine would eventually lead to the Finger Lakes, where Charles Fournier and Konstantin Frank were ready for the challenge.

Dr. Frank had proven that Vinifera grapes could be grown successfully in the cold weather climate of the Finger Lakes. This revelation inspired Bill Wagner and other pioneer Seneca Lake wineries to plant Vinifera grapes.

To break down Vinifera grapes one step further, I will speak about a special classification of Vinifera grapes known as "Noble Grapes." If you Google "noble grapes," you will find sites where "experts" tell you there are 6 or 7 Noble Grapes, or 7 Noble Grapes to as many as 18. The six that you will see first in every list are Chardonnay, Riesling, Sauvignon Blanc, Merlot, Cabernet, and Pinot Noir. The Vinifera grapes planted at Wagner Vineyards are Chardonnay, Riesling, Merlot, Cabernet Franc, Cabernet Sauvignon, Pinot Noir, and Gewürztraminer.

It is thought that the above grapes were classified as "noble" because of France's King Louis XIV, also known as "The Sun King." With the exception of the German Riesling, all of the noble grapes originated in France. The Riesling grape earned its place on the list because it is grown extensively in the Alsace Region of France, which produces world-class Rieslings.

King Louis' extravagant lifestyle was unparalleled in Europe. He ruled France for 72 years, living in such great luxury that most Europeans envied and wanted to copy the ways of the French. That meant consuming French wines. During Louis' reign, from 1643 to 1715, the improving quality of French wines brought them to other European countries, where they became widespread and highly sought. They were called "cépage noble," or roughly, "Noble Grapes."

Today, a "Noble grape" is simply an internationally recognized grape that produces high quality wine. Eleven of Wagner Vineyards' top selling wines are Noble Vinifera grapes. These are the grapes and wines that we will explore.

I will examine each of the Wagner Vineyards Noble grapes and, thus, the wines. Many chapters refer to an appendix, where an in-depth explanation of the wine term in question is explained. I strongly advise you to go to the proper appendix and read the article as you progress through the related chapters. Because of my food background, at the end of each chapter I have included suggested food and cheese pairings for the wine discussed.

At the end of this book, you will find a small cookbook. These are recipes that I used at my restaurant or in my catering business. Each recipe is paired with a Wagner wine. Many of the recipes include a Wagner wine in the ingredients.

Read on and enjoy!

Chapter Two: Riesling, from the Mosel to King (and Queen) of the Finger Lakes

I daily tell multitudes of wine consumers who step into my inner sanctum at Wagner Vineyards that the beautiful Seneca Lake viewed from our windows is the 15th deepest lake in the United States, a country with over 100,000 lakes.

Like the other Finger Lakes, Seneca Lake was formed by glaciers over two million years ago. The glaciers began to recede about 10,000 years ago, leaving shale and limestone soils with various types of clay, and steep hills overlooking the eleven lakes. John Wagner, who, along with his sister Laura, co-owns Wagner Vineyards, explained to me that our vineyards are situated primarily on Honeoye loam soil.

The word "Honeoye" is from the Iroquois "Hay-e-a-yeah." Legend has it that a Seneca brave was bitten by a rattlesnake, had to cut off the bitten finger, and later described the location of the incident as the place 'where the finger lies.' These productive soils occur on about 500,000 acres in New York State. Honeoye soils are fertile, have a high base saturation throughout, and are slightly acidic at the surface and neutral in the subsoil.

According to the United States Department of Agriculture Natural Resources Conservation Services:

> The Honeoye series consists of very deep, well-drained soils formed in glacial till which is strongly influenced by limestone and calcareous shale. They are nearly level to very steep soils on convex upland till plains and drumlins. The Honeoye soil is in the Alfisols soil order and is classified as fine-loamy, mixed, active, mesic Glossic Hapludalfs.

To honor this natural resource, New York unofficially named Honeoye as the "State Soil."

The Finger Lakes sit on nearly the 43rd parallel. Summers are hot and winters can be frigidly cold. Running through the 50th parallel in Germany is the Mosel (Moselle) River. The Mosel stretches from its beginnings in the French Vosges along the Luxembourg border for almost 320 miles. More than 150 of those miles twist through Germany before finally flowing into the Rhine on its way to the North Sea.

There are two primary types of slate soil found in the Mosel Valley: blue slate and red slate. Although both soils are relatively poor, the red soil areas generally have more clay, producing a richer, more lush style of Riesling, whereas blue slate wines are generally more floral.

Clayish slate and greywacke soil dominate much of the Mosel. (Greywacke is a type of soil with colored sedimentary sandstone that has been formed by river deposits mixed with rock fragments, quartz, compacted clay and feldspar.) It is a good soil for vineyards because of its rich mineral content and drainage capacity.

Thus, the thin soils of the Mosel are dominated by slate, shale, and clay.

Reference.com describes the similarity of shale of the Finger Lakes and the slate of the Mosel:

Shale is a sedimentary rock while slate is a metamorphic rock formed from shale. (The process of metamorphism does not melt the rocks, but instead transforms them into denser, more compact rocks. New minerals are created either by rearrangement of mineral components or by reactions with fluids that enter the rocks. Pressure or temperature can even change previously metamorphosed rocks into new types. Metamorphic rocks are often squished, smeared out, and folded. Despite these uncomfortable conditions, metamorphic rocks do not get hot enough to melt, or they would become igneous rocks!

Slate is much more durable than shale, due to the metamorphic process it undergoes. Slate and shale are similar in appearance. Visually, it can be hard to tell the two apart. Both types of rock break apart in layers and both types of rock also come in the same set of colors, with shades ranging from gray to black. The biggest difference, noticeable when handling the rocks, is in both the hardness and the different uses for each of the two unique types of rock.

Shale is the softer of the two rocks. It has a clay-like texture. In some cases, it is actually crushed and mixed with water to make types of clay, such as terracotta. Shale is also used in construction, where it is combined with limestone and then heated in order to make concrete and blocks. Finally, shale is a rich source of natural gas and oil.

In addition to similar soils, the climate of the two regions, which are very close to the same parallel, is very similar. The Mosel does not get as hot in the summer or as cold in the winter as the Finger Lakes can; but, overall, the climates are nearly identical. Seneca Lake has steep hills overlooking the lake as it stretches some 37 miles from Geneva to Watkins Glen. As the Mosel enters Germany, it twists and turns its way to the Rhine and has the steepest slopes in the wine world. More than half of the Mosel vineyards have inclines of over 30°. One vineyard, Bremmer Calmont, has inclines of over 60°. Workers must be lowered by ropes to work the vineyards, the vineyard work being done entirely by hand.

The hills surrounding Seneca Lake are not nearly as steep as those of the Mosel, but are still steep enough to enhance the microclimate of this region to produce world class Rieslings. The similar climate, soil, and geography of both regions are the Terroirs of the regions. **(See Appendix II)**

Many of the customers I meet at Wagner Vineyards are first-time visitors to the Finger Lakes. Most of those newbies have no idea what the most popular grape in our region is. I confess that I take "a few" liberties when I direct them to look out at Seneca Lake. I tell them that "Seneca Lake has very steep sides. In some places, it is a mile wide, with shale, limestone, and clay soil. It is on the 43rd parallel and today in the Finger Lakes it will be 78°F and partly cloudy. Then, I tell them, in western Germany runs the Mosel River. It has very steep sides, it is a mile across in some places, with shale, limestone and clay soil. It is on the 50th parallel and today in the Mosel it is 78°F and partly cloudy. Does that sound familiar? That is where God put the Riesling grape on Day 3 of Creation. Because the grape was brought to the Finger Lakes in 1958 by Dr. Frank, no one in this country does better Riesling than the Finger Lakes." They now know what grape made this region so famous.

The Finger Lakes Region does not share the same "terroir" with California's Napa Valley. A Napa Riesling does not compare favorably with a Finger Lakes Riesling, while some would say that a Finger Lakes Merlot does not compare favorably with a Napa Merlot. An "appellation" is the geographical name under which a wine grower is authorized to identify and market wine. In 1980, the Tax and Trade Bureau (TTB), a component of the US Department of the Treasury, began to assign official names to these wine appellations. The TTB established these distinct appellations as American Viticultural Areas (AVAs).

At the time I wrote this book, there were 246 AVAs in 33 states. More than half (139) of the AVAs are in California; Sonoma County alone contains 17 AVAs. AVAs vary widely in size, ranging from the Upper Mississippi River Valley AVA, with more than 19 million acres, with vineyards in four states, to the Cole Ranch AVA in Mendocino County, California, with only 60 acres. A region petitions the TTB when seeking AVA status. If the TTB agrees, it establishes the boundaries for the new AVA.

According to WineInstitute.org:

> When a U.S. winery wants to tell you the geographic
> pedigree of its wine, it uses a tag on its label called an
> Appellation of Origin. Appellations are defined either by
> political boundaries, such as the name of a county, state
> or country, or by federally-recognized regions called
> American Viticultural Areas (AVAs).
>
> In order for a wine to be assigned an Appellation of Origin
> defined by a political boundary, such as a county name for
> example, federal law requires that 75 percent or more of
> grapes used to make the wine be from that appellation,
> and that the wine be fully finished within the state in
> which the county is located.
>
> If a wine is designated with the name of an American
> Viticultural Area (AVA), federal regulations require that
> 85 percent or more of the wine is derived from grapes
> grown within the boundaries of that TTB-established AVA
> and that the wine is fully finished within the state or one
> of the states in which the AVA is located. Certain states
> have stricter standards for use of the name of an
> Appellation/AVA on wine labels.

Winery owners and winemakers often want their customers to know
what geographical area their wine comes from. An AVA on the bottle
will tell the buyer that a Riesling is from the Finger Lakes and not
Texas, or that a Merlot is from Napa and not Michigan.

As previously mentioned, the Sonoma Region of California has 17
distinct sub-AVAs within the Sonoma AVA. As you know, Wagner
Vineyards is located in the Finger Lakes. The Finger Lakes achieved
AVA status in 1982. There are 11,000 acres of grapevines in the Finger
Lakes AVA. Within the Finger Lakes AVA, wineries along both Seneca
and Cayuga lakes have been designated separate and distinct AVAs.
The Seneca Lake AVA was established in 1988 and contains
approximately 3,700 acres. Wagner Vineyards' 225 acres are located in

the Finger Lakes AVA, and more specifically in the Seneca Lake AVA. Because of the Seneca Lake Terroir, some of the finest Rieslings in the country come out of this AVA.

To summarize, God put the Riesling grape in the Mosel River Region. It is Germany's oldest wine region. The Mosel is a German wine appellation. When Dr. Frank brought the grape to the Finger Lakes in 1958, it flourished, because the terroir is nearly identical. The terroir of the Mosel appellation is almost identical to the terroir of the Finger Lakes appellation and more specifically to the Seneca Lake AVA appellation within the Finger Lakes appellation. (See map of the Finger Lakes Region at the beginning of Chapter One.)

Wagner Vineyards currently has one of the oldest Riesling vineyards in the region, and more planted Riesling vines than any other vineyard on Seneca Lake. Wagner Vineyards' 42-year-old Riesling vineyard still produces wonderful fruit; its grapes are used in our sweetest Riesling.

The Taste of Riesling

It doesn't take extensive research of the Riesling grape to discover the many similar descriptions of the taste that one should get from a good Riesling. As mentioned in my introduction, I won't tell a customer what fruits they should be tasting. I *will* tell them that a Riesling is fruity and that a wine like Gewürztraminer tends to be floral—but I will not suggest a particular fruit or flower. I will also tell people that the tingle they get in the back of their mouth is the high acid of the Riesling grape and wine. (Much more about acid later.)

As I wrote in my introduction, I refuse to use the term "minerality," but you would not easily find a description of the taste of a Riesling without seeing that term. Because of that, I invite you to turn to **Appendix III** and read my take on "minerality" before you go further with the description of the taste of a Riesling.

While you are educating yourself about the seemingly innocuous term, minerality, please also read about "acidity" in **Appendix IV**.

You are now ready for a rather common description of the taste of a Riesling from the Schmitt Söhne, the world's leading importer of Riesling.

More than 200 years ago, the Schmitts' ancestors settled in the small village of Longuich, located along the Mosel River, where they began to manage vineyards and produce wine.

> *According to Schmitt.Söhne.com: Some people think of Riesling as a sweet wine, but that would be like saying all chocolate is sweet, rather than coming in the variety of styles it actually does. True, most Riesling is crisp and fruity. But the taste profile can range from very dry to very sweet depending on the ripeness of the fruit and the style the winemaker is looking for. Mixed in with Riesling's fruit flavors (usually apple, peach and pear) and floral aromas is balanced acidity giving the wine its crisp, mouthwatering character and minerality adding complexity to the wine.*

> *The flavor of the Riesling grape is influenced like no other by the soil in which it's grown. The uniquely slate-heavy soils of Germany's wine growing regions impart a pronounced mineral character.*

> *This perfect balance of fruit and acidity, combined with a rich mineral base, makes German Rieslings unique among wines—red or white—from around the world.*

> *As previously mentioned, the degree to which Riesling grapes are allowed to ripen, known as selective harvesting, greatly influences their flavor. Most Riesling grapes are harvested early when they're light in character, then pressed and fermented.*

Now, armed with this general information, and remembering that the Finger Lakes have been named by USA Today as the Number One Wine Region in America, and also remembering that, for the last 20+ years, the best Rieslings in America have come from the Finger Lakes, just how good and how well-received are the Rieslings from Wagner Vineyards?

The tasting menu at Wagner's features many Rieslings. There are two dry Rieslings, a semi-dry Riesling, a rather sweet Riesling, a Riesling blend, a sparkling Riesling, and a Riesling Ice/Dessert wine. There are approximately 140 wineries in the Finger Lakes.

There are almost 400 wineries in New York State. These wineries are supported by the New York Wine and Grape Foundation. The Foundation was formed in 1985 by a New York State statute to support the wine industry's growth through investments in promotion, research, and capacity. Today, the Foundation's public-private partnership drives the industry's growth and makes it a major economic force that generates more than $5.5 billion in direct economic impact in the state.

Each year, the Foundation sponsors the New York Wine Classic, which has come to be known as "The Oscars" of the New York wine industry. The 2019 Classic featured 883 New York wines. The 21 judges include wine writers, wine educators, retailers, restaurateurs, and other experts from New York State and across the country. All samples are judged "blind" on their own merits, with "Winery of the Year" and other awards announced as soon as possible after the conclusion of the competition.

The Wagner Vineyards 2017 Dry Riesling, Semi-Dry Riesling, Riesling Select (our sweetest non-ice Riesling), and Riesling Ice all received Double Golds from the judges, more Double Gold Medals than any other winery. (The Double Gold is the highest award a wine can receive in any world competition.) Wagner Vineyards was also named New York State's "Winery of the Year." The Dry Riesling was declared Best Dry Riesling, Best Overall Riesling, and BEST WHITE WINE in the State of New York.

A week or so later, Wine Enthusiasts Magazine published their annual list of "Top 100 Best Buy Wines in the World." The Wagner Dry Riesling appeared as the 64th Best Buy wine *in the world*. Then, a few weeks before Thanksgiving, Oprah Winfrey's "O Magazine" named Wagner's Dry Riesling one of the "20 Affordable Best Wines for Thanksgiving."

Wagner Vineyards' 2018 Caywood East Riesling was rated 92 points by Wine Enthusiasts and called an *Editor's Choice* as one of the best Rieslings in the United States. Both the 2018 Caywood and the 2018 Wagner Dry Riesling were rated 93 by top sommeliers and wine directors in the USA at the 2020 Sommeliers Choice Awards.

How well received are the Wagner Rieslings? They are considered to be among the best in the United States.

Food and Riesling

Stacy Slinkard of "The Spruce Eats" writes: "One of Riesling's key pairing privileges comes via sheer variety. Today's wine shelves spotlight an impressive array of regional Rieslings, with a variety of sweet to dry options, light to full-bodied bottles and specific regional-based terroir influences. Rieslings are known for their remarkable balance between acidity and sugar. It's the acidity that allows it to encounter and woo a variety of difficult plate pairing partners.

"The acid allows the wine to handle hearty sauces, high-end meats, and even lighter fare like appetizers while simultaneously offsetting the tangy flavors of ginger and lime in Asian fare. Riesling's innate fruit factor (apple, pear, citrus, and tropical) and personal preferences for sweeter styles make this wine a natural for taming the heat of spicier food with a touch of palate sweet."

Between my catering business and time working at various wineries, I've spent a great deal of time researching a common question: Which wines should be paired with which foods?

I find that Riesling pairs with more types of foods than any other wine. It is one of those wines that, because of its acidity and its taste of fruit, really brings balance to almost any table. As mentioned, Riesling has the highest acidity of any white grape, and acid is important in choosing a wine to pair with a dish. Spicy Mexican, Indian, or Thai food? Riesling is the answer. It can also soften the acid already in a dish like a lemony Chicken French, and can cut through fatty sauces created with eggs and cheeses. As an added benefit, the acidity actually helps cleanse your palate between bites.

Other than the above descriptions, and in addition to the foods already listed, and without further ado, I suggest pairing Rieslings with fried or baked fish, simple seafood dishes, cream sauces, butter sauces, sautéed mushrooms, roasted chicken, grilled pork chops, charcuterie, crab cakes, roasted meats with pan sauce, and roasted vegetables.

Cheeses: Ricotta, Jarlsberg, Camembert, Gruyere.
(See COOKBOOK for suggested recipes to complement Reisling wines.)

Chapter Three: The Unique Taste of Gewürztraminer

In the introduction to this book, I mentioned the years I spent researching the background and history of the grapes and wines that I pour. This research allows me to present wines a bit differently from anyone else. Both nearby Cornell University and the University of California at Davis have been breaking down and analyzing the DNA structure of grapes for more than 20 years.

It is fairly easy to discover the DNA origins of many grapes. Gewürztraminer is not one of them. There are several different schools of thought concerning the origins of this intriguing grape and the wine produced from it.

Let me begin the discussion of Gewürztraminer in a very strange place. Let's start in the southeastern provinces of Guangdong and Fugian in China. There, a native tropical tree produces lychees, a fruit which has been cultivated since the 11th Century. A tall evergreen tree, the lychee bears small fleshy fruits inside an inedible, reddish, roughly textured skin or shell. This spiky shell covers a sweet flesh used in many different Asian dessert dishes. (The juice and fruit also appear in lychee-tinis.) The fleshy fruits, also known as "lychee nuts," have the floral aroma of rose petals and a sweet flavor. Any accurate description of the taste of Gewürztraminer includes mention of the lychee fruit.

The term, "aromatic" appears in virtually every description of Gewürztraminer. Like "full bodied" and "minerality," aromatic is one of the terms that you may think you understand, but which you probably wouldn't be able to define if challenged. So let's just say that if it is aromatic, it has a "pleasant and distinctive smell." Of course, what is pleasant and distinctive to one person is not necessarily pleasant and distinctive to someone else. The primary aromatic descriptors applied to Gewürztraminer are typically lychee, rose petal, tropical fruit and perfume.

After the smell—or the "nose"—of your Gewürztraminer, there is the taste. On the palate, it is marked by its full texture, low acidity, and spicy, possibly gingery or cinnamon flavors.

If you have been a longtime whiskey drinker and enjoy rye, bourbon, and Canadian whiskeys, imagine your first taste of peat-based Scotch whiskey. You would immediately notice a drastic change in taste. For most people, the Scotch is an acquired taste. If you drink vodka and then switch to gin, you will probably need to "acquire" the taste of the unfamiliar beverage.

Imagine being a lifelong tea-drinker and switching to coffee. You would probably have to acquire a taste for the unfamiliar flavor of coffee. The process is much the same when you taste a Gewürztraminer after spending years consuming Chardonnay, Riesling and Sauvignon Blanc, or other wines with a fruit style finish. For many, the spicy, floral finish is an "acquired taste." I always pour a taste of fruity Riesling before I pour a taste of Gewürztraminer, so you can experience the remarkable difference between the fruitiness of most white wines and the uniquely flavored Gewürztraminer.

I often talk about the world's ancient grapes. The list always includes Pinot Noir, Gouais Blanc, and Savagnin (not to be confused with Sauvignon—as in Sauvignon Blanc and Cabernet Sauvignon). Today, Savagnin Blanc is grown almost exclusively in France's Jura Region and is used to make Vin Jaune. "This wine is matured in barrels for several years under a naturally occurring film of flor yeast. During this maturation period the wine develops rich, nutty flavors. It also gains the deep yellow color which gives it its name." (*Wine-Searcher.com*) (Flor is the veil or thin layer of yeast cells that forms on the surface of of the wine.)

This is where it starts to get confusing. There are basically two schools of thought about the family of Traminer grapes (which included Savagnin) and Gewürztraminer.

South Tyrol, a province that was formerly part of southwestern Austria, is situated in the Alps, where it occupies the extreme northeastern part of the "Italian Boot." (South Tyrol was handed over to Italy following World War I.) The village of Tramin lies within South Tyrol.

The Traminer family of grapes is named after the village of Tramin, where this family of grapes supposedly had its roots, literally and figuratively. The Traminer family of grapes can be traced to this region between the 11th and 16th centuries, a period of 500 years. This family of grapes includes Auvernat Blanc, Bon Blanc, Forment, Fromenteau, Gentil Blanc, Schleitheimer, Ryvola Bila, and Savagnin. Most likely, you have never heard of these grapes, although Savagnin is nearly universally thought to be one of the oldest grapes in the world. DNA research published in 2019 confirmed that a 900-year-old grape seed found in Orléans, in central France, was genetically identical to modern Savagnin Blanc. This is evidence that the variety has been farmed for at least that long, using cuttings derived from one ancestral plant.

The Traminer family of grapes is so genetically unstable that DNA experts do not always agree on the true original source of these grapes. White Traminer and the aforementioned Savagnin are now considered by many to be the same grape. Popular Bordeaux grapes, such as Cabernet Sauvignon and Merlot, contain traces of Traminer in their DNA.

The first school of thought asserts that the Traminer family of grapes began in the village of Tramin, in the province of South Tyrol, and then migrated into Germany and France, courtesy of traveling monks or the conquering Romans, or both. Savagnin probably mutated in France.

The second school contends that the Traminer strain of grapes began in France and Germany, and was later spread to Tramin by the monks and/or Romans, where, over time, the grapes acquired the name, Traminer. Remember that seed from Orléans, France, is genetically dated to about 900 years ago; records indicate that Traminer grapes were being cultivated in South Tyrol at about the same time.

This background now brings us to the grape in question: Gewürztraminer. Gewürztraminer's DNA is universally believed be a mutation of Savignin that was formed in the Alsace Region of France. For years, I have said that it was believed that traveling German monks found the Gewürztraminer grape in the Alsace Region of France. The monks brought the grape to their home in the German-speaking province of South Tyrol, in southern Austria. (Gewurz is the German word for "spice," thus "Spice-Tramin-er" or Gewürztraminer.) But that may not be the true origin of this grape. It seems that the Traminer or Savagnin grape migrated *to* the Alsace Region of France. The unstable nature of this family of grapes then produced a mutation of the Savagnin grape, a pink-skinned grape with highly floral flavors that eventually made its way back to Tramin. In keeping with its origins, Gewürztraminer is best-known and most successful in France's Alsace Region, but it is also prominent in Germany and northern Italy (South Tyrol).

There is some recent conjecture that Gewürztraminer could have mutated in the village of Tramin, but I am sticking with my original story, that the monks brought it to Tramin. (Yes, that is my "final answer"!)

Traminer grapes seem to have adapted well to the region in which they were planted. Remember, traveling monks and conquering Romans would uproot and transplant grapes from one region to another. Traminer grapes seem to be very flavorful and aromatic, while also pungent to the nose, and to be differently colored from the green color of most white grapes.

The Traminer grape doesn't have much of a New World presence, as it prefers cool climates, but it has found a home in the Finger Lakes, California and Washington.

I have found the Wagner Gewürztraminer wines (Dry and Semi-Dry) to not be overly floral or perfumey, unlike many others in the Finger Lakes. They retain their unique taste, which is distinctly different from the fruit-based Rieslings, but not to the extent of turning one off to their finish as tasting too perfumey.

Food and Gewürztraminer

I opened this dialogue by comparing the "nose" and taste of Gewürztraminer to rose petals and lychees. So, what in the world do you eat with rose petals and lychees?

Just as no description of Gewürztraminer is found without incorporating "lychee," no discussion of pairing Gewürztraminer with food is found without mentioning spicy Asian dishes.

American Gewürztraminers tend to be drier than their European counterparts, thus pairing well with Asian food, particularly Chinese, Indian and Thai. Gewürztraminer generally benefits from dishes with more than a touch of sweetness and heat, such as Sichuan Chinese and dishes with ginger.

As many know, Gewürztraminer is considered by many to be the go-to wine for Thanksgiving. It pairs beautifully with pumpkin, most winter squash, sweet potatoes and much of the other traditional Thanksgiving fare.

Suggested cheeses: Muenster and soft cow milk cheeses.

Chapter Four: The Many Tastes of Chardonnay

Chardonnay is, quite simply, the most popular white wine on Earth. The Chardonnay grape is grown in more wine regions than any other grape in the world. You would be hard pressed to find a wine region that does *not* grow at least some Chardonnay grapes.

In Chapter Two: Riesling, I referred you to Appendix II, which explains terroir and microclimate. Terroir is the set of factors (climate, weather, soil, geography) that creates the character of wine and its features, and which distinguishes a Chardonnay from the Burgundy Region from the Napa Region from the Finger Lakes Region. Chardonnay is one of the very few grapes that thrives in widely varied terroirs, resulting in very different and complex tastes. Chardonnay adapts to virtually any climate, any weather, and any soil.

Around 50 BC, the Romans attacked the Gauls and added France to the growing Roman Empire. Following each of their conquests, the Romans were known to plant something from their native (or previously acquired) soil in the newly conquered territory. They planted the Pinot Noir grape, one of the three oldest grapes in the world, in what is today the Burgundy Region of France. (See Chapter 7: Pinot Noir.) It is believed that, years later, the Romans brought the Gouais Blanc grape—also one of the world's oldest grapes and nearly extinct today—from Croatia and added it to France's Burgundy Region.

The village of Chardonnay lies within the southern region of Burgundy and is thought to be over 1000 years old. The name "Chardonnay" originally meant "place of thistles" or "thistle covered place." The cross pollination of Pinot Noir and Gouais Blanc that likely created the Chardonnay grape probably happened there. As with many other of today's world-famous grapes, the Chardonnay grape was probably shared throughout the region by monks and the Romans. In today's wine world and on the shelves in your local liquor store, Pinot Noir is Burgundy, while Chardonnay is White Burgundy.

The Cistercian monks wrote about the Chardonnay grape as early as 1300 AD. It is believed that they brought the Chardonnay grape to Chablis, an area in the northernmost region of Burgundy, in the late 1200s. (The Cistercian monks were a French order of monks that was founded in 1098.)

All Chablis wine is made *entirely* from Chardonnay grapes. Despite potential damage from spring frost, the cool climate of the Chablis Region lends itself to the high acidity in Chablis wines. (Remember that, in the Burgundy Region, Chardonnay is known as both Chablis and White Burgundy.) The soil of the Chablis Region further allows winemakers to emphasize the region's terroir to create a Chardonnay (Chablis) that is different from other Chardonnays (White Burgundies) in the Burgundy Region and in France.

While the Finger Lakes were formed by glaciers "only" about a million years ago, France's Burgundy Region is believed to have been a tropical sea more than *200* million years ago. It is not uncommon to find fossilized sea urchins in the limestone that was deposited by the ancient sea.

Many Chardonnays of the Burgundy Region are described as having "zesty minerality" due to the limestone left in the rich Burgundy soil. As with many highly acidic wines, the high acid in a Chablis mellows with age. Because of this, some of the world's oldest examples of aged Chardonnays are Chablis wines.

The French describe the raw flavors of a ripe Chablis as having "flinty" notes, to be "steely," with the smell and taste as a "wet stone." In this country we refer to this effect as "minerality." (I much prefer the use of the terms "wet stone" and "steely" to "minerality.") Because the acidity mellows over time, most White Burgundies, including Chablis, benefit from bottle age. Bottled Chablis has been known to improve over time, for as long as 15 years.

Earlier in this book, I told you that when I pour wine, I don't tell my customers what kinds of fruit they "should" notice. Not everyone will taste the same thing. In the previous chapter on Gewürztraminer, I listed some of the things that are often mentioned when describing that grape, such as the lychee fruit and rose petals. In addition to "wet flint rocks," Chardonnay that is unoaked (as it is in most of Europe and South America, and now making a huge comeback in the United States) someone, somewhere will taste and smell lemon, apple and pear in the cooler climates. In warmer climates pineapple, passionfruit, peach and melon are referenced. In the hottest climates, people may taste fig, banana, and mango.

Broadly, White Burgundy can be found in four production areas within the Burgundy Region. Each of these areas has a different terroir and characteristics and, thus, different flavor profiles.

The Chablis Region is one of these four production areas. The others are Bourgogne Blanc, Mâconnais, and the Côte de Beaune. Of these four regions, only the Côte de Beaune features Chardonnay fermented in oak. The others feature unoaked Chardonnay.

From the opening discussion of terroir and how it affects the taste of Chardonnay grapes, I have basically been talking about grapes fermented with no oak influence. These *unoaked* Chardonnays will differ in flavor, reflecting the region in which they were grown.

The process of "oaking" Chardonnay began in the Côte de Beaune Region. WineFolly.com refers to these Chardonnays as the "crème de la crème" of White Burgundy. "These wines are typically oak-aged, with rich, fleshy, yellow apple and star fruit flavors with undertones of truffle, hazelnut and vanilla."

Wine Folly goes on to say that "the Côte de Beaune is the Beverly Hills of White Burgundy production, and is home to some of the most expensive vineyard land on Earth. The roughly 25 Kilometer (~15$^{1/2}$ miles) strip of the Côte de Beaune produces some of the most show-stopping, intense expressions of the Chardonnay on the planet."

Chardonnay in the New World and the Finger Lakes

We learned about Dr. Frank and Charles Fournier in Chapter One. Because Chardonnay adapts to virtually any terroir, it was one of the first grapes planted east of the Rocky Mountains. As I will explain, Chardonnay is one of the main ingredients of Champagne.

Fournier wanted to make a world class Champagne. And he succeeded! By the late 1950s, they harvested the first Vinifera grapes for sale in eastern North America. Chardonnay went on to become a staple in the Finger Lakes Region of New York which, like the Burgundy Region of France, provides the cool climate in which these grapes thrive.

We have seen that Chardonnay can do well in almost any climate, but it is particularly well-suited to New York's Finger Lakes.

Chardonnay is a late-budding grape, which reduces the likelihood of damage from a crippling spring frost. Cool nights, combined with the fact that Chardonnay grapes remain on the vine a little longer, allow the grapes to achieve higher sugar levels than grapes produced in warmer climates.

I've already discussed the flavors of Chardonnay. They are basically the same in the Finger Lakes as in France. Warmer climate Chardonnays (in California, for example) may have less of a fruit-forward taste and more honey, butterscotch, and, according to some, nutty oily flavors.

Speaking of California, in the 1970s, winemakers from California visited the Côte de Beaune area of Burgundy, where they fell in love with the oaked Chardonnays. They brought the practice of oaking the wine back to California and, in the process, changed the way America tastes and appreciates Chardonnay.

By the 1980s, heavily oaked California Chardonnays became an American phenomenon. In addition to the oak taste, a malolactic fermentation was added. **(See Appendix V)** This taste is not to be confused with the taste that comes from the oak itself. If you have read the appendix article concerning malolactic fermentation, you know that, by changing the malic acid in a grape to lactic acid, the wine will acquire a buttery taste.

America has slowly tired of heavily oaked Chardonnays. The taste of any fruit was absent. Many people tasted just vanilla, cinnamon and butter. The butter taste was so overwhelming that people described a sip of Chardonnay as tasting a "butter bomb." The slogan, "ABC" was born: *"Anything But Chardonnay!"*

In the last decade or so, the American wine consumer has begun to rediscover Chardonnay. Unoaked Chardonnay has made a comeback in this country and in the Finger Lakes. A shorter time in oak allows the fruit of the grape to shine again, in the style of Côte de Beaune, leading to a resurgence of Chardonnay in the United States.

Wagner Vineyards has more than 8 acres of Chardonnay grapes. In 2019, they harvested over 5,500 gallons of these grapes for use in their own wine production. The Wagners produce 3 distinct Chardonnays. Customers are able to taste one that is totally unoaked, having spent approximately 8 months in stainless steel.

With the resurgence of unoaked Chardonnay in the United States (and in the Finger Lakes), the Wagner Unoaked Chardonnay is the best-selling of the three varieties produced at the winery. It has become one of the top 5 selling wines in the Wagner profile of 32 wines. In a July 2018 article titled, "Unoaked Chardonnay Deserves Your Respect," One of this country's leading wine websites, Vinepair.com, named the Wagner 2017 Unoaked Chardonnay as one of the top five unoaked Chardonnays in America.

Probably more than any other grape (or wine), Chardonnay lends itself to the winemaker and his or her approach to creating the final outcome. Think of an artist who has a plentiful palette of different colors to create a work of art. The "palette of colors" available to a winemaker to create a Chardonnay is also plentiful. If you will forgive the wordplay, Chardonnay grapes provide a palette for your palate!

Chardonnay can be fermented in stainless steel. It can be lightly fermented in oak, after spending time in stainless steel. Or it can be totally fermented in oak. The winemaker may use new barrels or a combination of old and new barrels. Those barrels may be fire bent or water bent. **(See Appendix VI)** In addition, the Chardonnay can go through a malolactic fermentation process, adding buttery aromas to the wine. The wine may be left to sit on the dead yeast cells (lees) in either the steel tank or in the barrel. "Sitting on the lees" can lend a taste of biscuits or dough to the wine.

Meet the Wagner Artists

So, overlooking beautiful Seneca Lake from the Wagner Vineyards deck, let's bring in ten "artists." If you give them identical palettes of paints, the result will be ten *similar* paintings with ten distinctive interpretations of the view of Seneca Lake, employing a wide variety of colors.

Now, suppose you have 5,500 gallons of Chardonnay. Some of it goes directly to stainless steel; the remainder is allowed to age and ferment in a variety of barrels in the barrel cellar. Your palette of "paint" (barrels) now consists of barrels of different ages, some water bent, some fire bent, as well as the other options of using malolactic fermentation and allowing or not allowing the wine to "sit on the lees." Ten winemakers will create ten different wines using a combination of the various barrels and techniques available to them. That is the art of winemaking, and the reason that Chardonnay can have so many different tastes from so many regions and terroirs.

The two remaining Wagner Chardonnays spend varying amounts of time in those barrels. The Barrel Fermented Chardonnay spends its entire pre-bottled life in fire- or water bent barrels of different ages. The Wagner Reserve Chardonnay is a more crafted Chardonnay, combining Chardonnay from the stainless tanks and the varied oak barrels. The true artistry of our winemakers is exposed as their "palette of paints" creates two unique Wagner Chardonnays.

Food and Chardonnay

The many styles of Chardonnay pair with many styles of food.

For unoaked, cool climate Chardonnay (Chablis and Finger Lakes unoaked Chardonnays), I recommend crab, lobster, oysters, scallops, shrimp, steamed or grilled fish, chicken, vegetables, creamy soups and pastas.

For fruitier unoaked or lightly oaked Chardonnays and Chardonnays from warmer climates: Caesar salad, ham, salmon, chicken, pork, or pasta in a heavy cream sauce.

For barrel-fermented, barrel aged or "reserve" Chardonnays, I recommend eggs; steak béarnaise, grilled veal chops with mushrooms; red peppers, corn, butternut squash and pumpkin, cheddar cheese.

Cheeses to pair with unoaked Chardonnay: mild, semi-soft cheeses like goat, Stilton, and Fontina.

For oaked Chardonnay: sharp cheddar and blue cheese.

Chapter Five: Cabernet Franc and the Bordeaux

And now for some reds!

For the most part, white wines are chilled and finish with a fruity taste. They are harvested and pressed early in the day, and the juice is in fermentation tanks before lunch. It can take less than a year to go from harvest to store shelves.

Red grapes and wines are a totally different "animal." Instead of the fruit finish of a white wine, a red wine finishes dry, bitter, and astringent.

The juice of nearly all red grapes is white. Squeeze any of our Bordeaux or Pinot Noir grapes and you get clear, "white" juice. (There is a classification of red grapes known as Teinturier. It includes Alicante Bouschet, Chambourein, and Saperavi. The juice of those three grapes is red.)

While white grapes are crushed and the juice sent immediately to the fermenters, red grapes remain in the huge bins where the harvester has deposited them. The bins hold nearly a ton of freshly harvested grapes. At Wagner Vineyards, the bins are taken to a warehouse, where yeast is added and the wine making process begins.

For the next week, the staff stands on top of the bins, and "punches" the grapes with a long pole that has a large flat surface at the end, two to three times a day. (This process replaces the hilarious grape-stomping scene in one of the best-known episodes of the 1950s TV show, *I Love Lucy!* It is well worth watching or re-watching.)

At the end of the week, the formerly clear juice is now red from sitting on the dark red to black skins of the grapes. The skins and seeds contain an organic compound, tannin, which also becomes part of the juice/wine. **(See Appendix VII for a full explanation of** tannin.) After the week, the "wine" is pumped into a fermentation tank, where it may spend two months settling and fermenting all of the sugar from the juice/wine. It then goes into a variety of oak barrels, usually for a year or longer.

We are currently pouring a 2017 Cabernet Franc. Bud break (the first tiny bud) for this wine began on April 30, 2017. The grapes were harvested on October 23. The "punching" ended on November 3, when the wine was transferred to the fermentation tanks. The wine left the tanks two months later, on January 5, 2018, and entered the various barrels. The wine was bottled on January 13, 2019. (Note: the date on a bottle of wine is the date that the grape was harvested, not when it was bottled!) After bottling, the wine goes into "bottle shock" **(See Appendix VIII)** for several more months before it can be put on our shelves.

I love pouring our reds at Wagner Vineyards. Cabernet Franc, Cabernet Sauvignon, and Merlot can all be traced to the Bordeaux Region of France. They top the list of Vinifera red wines on our tasting menu and appear in that order. If you happen by my tasting bar and choose all red wines, as many do, you will hear this:

These first three wines all originally came from the same wine region in France. France is divided into 12 wine regions, including Bordeaux, Burgundy, Champagne, the Loire, Alsace, the Rhône, and more. Last year, the Bordeaux produced over 900,000,000 bottles of wine! (You read that correctly: *nine hundred million* bottles.) There are more than 300,000 acres of grapes in France's Bordeaux Region, owned by over 6,800 families. That is six times larger than our Napa Valley.

The Bordeaux is the largest wine region in the world. Remember, the grapes of the Bordeaux Region are Cabernet Franc, Cabernet Sauvignon, Merlot, Malbec—yes, Malbec (You want to say, "No Johnny, Malbec is from Argentina" but you would be wrong. Malbec is a Bordeaux grape that is *grown* in Argentina.)

The first vineyard you can see from our window is Cabernet Franc, a Bordeaux grape grown in the Finger Lakes. The fifth Bordeaux grape is

Petit Verdot, a blending grape that is grown all over the world. Carménère is the sixth of the red Bordeaux grapes. (Carménère is so similar to Merlot that, in Chile, they planted, harvested, fermented and bottled Carménère as "Merlot" for over 100 years before discovering its true identity in 1994!) It is not warm enough, long enough, in the Finger Lakes to successfully grow Malbec, Petit Verdot, or Carménère.

Of those grapes, Cabernet Franc was the first to enter the Bordeaux Region. It was brought to Bordeaux by the infamous Cardinal Richelieu in the early 1600s. (If you have the time, you really should read The Three Musketeers by Alexandre Dumas. Excepting his role in bringing Cabernet Franc grapes to Bordeaux, Richelieu was a pretty rotten guy.)

When Cabernet Franc was firmly established, Richelieu had it distributed to all the monasteries in the Bordeaux Region. A letter from the Cardinal, the head of the Catholic Church in France, simply commanded, "plant this grape." One hundred years later, Cabernet Franc dominated the Bordeaux Region.

Cabernet translates to "red grape" in French. "Franc" comes from the Latin, "Franconian Rex," King of the Francs. It was known as the king of the red grapes and it dominated France for almost 100 years. But if you go into any bar in the country and ask for a 'Cab,' no one ever asks, "Would you like Cabernet Franc or Cabernet Sauvignon?"

In the late 1600s, monks in an eastern Bordeaux monastery wrote about a "wild white" grape that had been in their vineyard for about thirty years. The seeds had probably been dropped by a bird. Before that, the monks did not have a white grape. They took care of it, propagated it, and after thirty years, next to their massive Cabernet Franc vineyard, they had a nice little vineyard of what they called the "wild white grape."

One of the words for "wild" in French is "sauvignon." The grape was Sauvignon Blanc and in the late 1600s, Cabernet Franc and Sauvignon Blanc cross-pollinated.

Just like apples and cherries, grapes open as flowers. In the late 1600s, a bee touched the male part of a Sauvignon Blanc flower and then flew over and touched the female part of a Cabernet Franc flower, and Cabernet Sauvignon was born.

Cabernet Franc has a peppery, spicy taste. You don't get that taste with Cabernet Sauvignon because half of its DNA is a white grape. Today, Cabernet Sauvignon is the most planted grape in the world.

God created grapes on Day Three. He created blackbirds on Day Four. Those blackbirds have been eating grapes ever since.

Blackbirds are a problem in every vineyard in the world. The monks wrote that the blackbirds had always been "equal-opportunity blackbirds" and attacked all of their vineyards at harvest time.

We know that the monks had at least five vineyards, maybe more. They had Cabernet Franc (of course), Cabernet Sauvignon, Malbec, Carménère and a grape you have never heard of. During a harvest season in the late 1700s, the blackbirds concentrated on one section of just one vineyard. The puzzled monks walked into the vineyard and found a larger, darker, redder grape than they had ever "noticed" before. I say "noticed" because God did not wake up one morning and make a new grape. The monks had been picking this grape for years, but didn't notice that it was different.

If I were to bring a cluster of Cabernet Franc, Cabernet Sauvignon and this grape from our vineyards and lay them on the bar and tell you what they were, then mix them up, they look so much alike that you would not be able to distinguish between them.

The monks had been picking this grape, the blackbirds' favorite, for years without noticing the difference.

With apologies to Cornell University, I have to say that the University of California at Davis is the Number One wine college in America. In 1997, they began breaking down DNA of the grapes from the Bordeaux. They began with Cabernet Sauvignon, thinking they knew the answer from the monks' writings. They determined that, yes, Cabernet Sauvignon was the result of cross pollination of Cabernet Franc and Sauvignon Blanc.

In 1998, they broke down the DNA of the current grape in question. (At this point, I usually hold up the bottle to avoid saying the name of the grape until the end.) The scientists were amazed to discover that it has five distinct DNA structures: Cabernet Franc, Cabernet Sauvignon, Malbec, Carménère, and one of the rarest of Bordeaux grapes that is almost extinct today.

The scientist at Davis found a DNA number for the grape, but didn't give it a name, just a number. Three years later, a French viticulturist gave a name to the number: Magdeleine.

Magdeleine is one of the earliest ripening red grapes, now grown in front of houses as a decorative vine. It is fully ripe on July 22nd, the feast day of Mary Magdalene. It is the DNA mother of our grape. Obviously, the monks knew nothing of DNA in the late 1700s. They grew grapes, drank wine and prayed. So when the monks named the grape, they named it after the bird that discovered it. In French, blackbird translated to "Merlot."

In early 2020, I actually poured for a gentleman who had worked in that lab at UC Davis after 1998. He told me that the story of breaking down the DNA of the Merlot grape is on the walls of the lab. They even have a picture of the French viticulturist who named the Magdeleine grape.

Here's a rough breakdown of the grape varietal plantings in the Bordeaux appellation for red wine in 2020. It shows a slight increase in Merlot and a decrease in Cabernet: Merlot, 66% (185,000 acres); Cabernet Sauvignon, 22.5% (63,000 acres); Cabernet Franc, 9.5% (27,000 acres).

Ninety-eight percent of all red wine grape varieties in the Bordeaux Region are dominated by the top three grape varietals. The same is true in the Finger Lakes. The remaining 2% of the entire Bordeaux wine region used in the production of red Bordeaux wine is devoted to three different grape varieties: Malbec (2,400 acres); Petit Verdot (1,200 acres); and Carménère (17 acres).

As you can see, Carménère is practically extinct in the Bordeaux wine region today.

The above treatise about the wines and their history is the result of extensive research, with some embellishing by me.

Now we'll look at each grape and wine individually. Since I'm not standing in front of you with bottles of Cabernet Franc, Cabernet Sauvignon, and Merlot for you to taste in order to distinguish their differences for yourself, I will tell you what the majority of the wine-consuming public thinks the three wines from the Bordeaux should taste like. You can use the descriptions as a guide or you can read past them and decide their differences for yourself.

What I *can* tell you is that they are different—noticeably different. So please bear with me as I break one of my own wine pouring rules, including in my breakdown of each wine, what the rest of the world thinks they taste like.

Cabernet Franc

Esteemed wine writer, Jancis Robinson, wrote:

> We've established that a Bordeaux blend consists of the grapes from the Bordeaux Region of France. Most Bordeaux blends contain Cabernet Franc, Cabernet Sauvignon, and Merlot. (Malbec, Petit Verdot, and rarely, Carménère are also used in Bordeaux blends.) There are over 6,000 wineries in the Bordeaux Region and you would be hard-pressed to find a single one that did not blend their grapes to create a Bordeaux blend, much like the wineries of the Finger Lakes do when making a Riesling.

Cabernet Franc is always introduced to customers with the description of a "peppery" finish. Fans of this Cabernet often describe its taste to include tobacco, raspberry, bell pepper, cassis (black currant), and violets, in addition to pepper. It proves to be a wonderful addition to other Bordeaux grapes in creating Bordeaux blends.

In most wine regions where it is grown, Cabernet Franc is used almost exclusively as part of a blend. It is bottled in cooler climates like the Loire of France and the Finger Lakes of New York where it thrives. It tends to bud a week earlier and ripen a week earlier than the popular Cabernet Sauvignon grape.

Many areas of France grow a little extra Cabernet Franc as an "insurance grape." Cabernet Sauvignon ripens so late that it sometimes must be picked early, because of frost, before is fully ripe. Cabernet Franc berries are quite small and blue-black in color, with fairly thin skins. As with Chardonnay, Cabernet Franc can adapt to a wide variety of vineyard soil types. However, it seems most comfortable in sandy, chalky soil. Its skin is thinner than that of its "child," Cabernet Sauvignon, and is generally thought to be less acidic than its more famous counterpart, with less tannin.

As mentioned before, you do not have to look far before finding a reference that, yes, the infamous Cardinal Richelieu discovered the Cabernet Franc grape in the Basque Region of France in the early 1600s. It is thought to have been originally cultivated at the Abbey of Bourgueil, in the Loire Valley, by a monk named Breton. For this reason, the original name for the wine produced from the Cabernet Franc grape was Breton. Parts of the modern-day middle Loire Region are still called Breton. Cabernet Francs from the Loire are considered to be some of the finest in the world.

In the mid 1600s, the Cabernet Franc grape made its way to the Libournais area of the Bordeaux Region. It continues to thrive today throughout the Bordeaux Region.

Food and Cabernet Franc

Cabernet Franc is great with dishes that are rich in herbs and tomatoes. If you like barbecue, you will adore Cabernet Franc. It pairs well with roasted pork, stews, spicy herbed meatballs with tomato sauce, and lamb. It is also great with mushrooms, eggplant, roasted red peppers, and spinach.

Cheeses: Goat cheese, Camembert, Feta, Fontina.

Chapter Six: Cabernet Sauvignon and Merlot

I suppose I should admit before I delve much further into my next wine, that I am not a big fan of Cabernet Sauvignon. I have no idea why, but I would rather order a Pinot or a Cab Franc, or even a Merlot, before I would order a "Cab." But I must give it its due, as it is the most popular wine in the world.

There are about 10,000 varieties of wine grapes in the world. Some of them are hybrids that never left the lab. Of those 10,000 grape varieties, the number one planted wine grape in the world is Cabernet Sauvignon.

It is also one of the world's *newest* Vinifera grapes. Remember, Cabernet Franc dominated France for almost one hundred years before it cross-pollinated with Sauvignon Blanc in the late 1600s. The DNA of Sauvignon Blanc can be traced to the southwest of France. (It is probably a descendent of the ancient Savagnin grape that you read about in the chapter on Gewürztraminer, and thus a member of the Traminer family.) It grew wild or, as the French would say, "sauvage," and became known as the "wild white" grape, or today, Sauvignon Blanc. The bees did their cross-pollenating job sometime in the 17th Century, producing the most popular grape in the world today.

Later, you will read that the Pinot Noir grape is well over 2000 years old. Considering Cabernet Sauvignon's relative youth in the grape world, its rise to prominence is interesting.

> There are two key reasons for Cabernet Sauvignon's rise to dominance. The most simple and primordial of these is that its vines are highly adaptable to different soil types and climates; it is grown at latitudes as disparate as 50°N (Okanagan in Canada) and 20°S (northern Argentina), and in soils as different as the Pessac-Leognan gravels and the iron-rich terra rossa of Coonawarra. Secondary to this,

but just as important, is that despite the diversity of terroirs in which the vine is grown, Cabernet Sauvignon wines retain an inimitable "Cab" character, nuanced with hints of provenance in the best-made examples. There is just a single reason, however, for the durability of the variety's fame and that is simple economics; the familiarity and marketability of the Cabernet Sauvignon name has an irresistible lure to wine companies looking for a reliable return on their investment. (Wine-Searcher.com)

Its amazing ability to adapt to so many different terroirs explains how the grape can produce great wine on multiple continents. France has the most plantings of Cabernet Sauvignon, as more than 136,000 acres are cultivated with Cabernet Sauvignon. After France, the greatest cultivated area of Cabernet Sauvignon is found in Chile, with over 100,000 acres, followed by the United States (nearly 90,000 acres), Australia (60,000+ acres), Spain (59,000 acres), and rounding out the top six, China (more than 57,000 acres).

The Cabernet Sauvignon grape is also widely cultivated in Italy, South Africa, Argentina and Bulgaria. It is planted in vineyards around the globe, from Canada to Lebanon to New Zealand to Israel and Austria. It does best in warmer climates, in vineyards that have a full day of sun and good drainage, which allows the roots to bury themselves deep into the soil.

Cabernet Sauvignon requires a longer growing season than Cabernet Franc and Merlot, and sometimes must be harvested before it is fully ripened. When harvested early, Cabernet Sauvignon tends to have aromas resembling green peppers like its DNA parent, Cabernet Franc, and not the aroma of thyme and tobacco leaf that Sauvignon is known for. As you know from Chapter 5: Cabernet Franc, I am not a fan of specifically describing what *you* will taste in a wine, so I usually rely on someone else to help me. WineCellarInsider.com says that, at its very best, a classic Cabernet Sauvignon produces wines with "deep, dark colors that offer complex scents and concentrated flavors ranging from blackberries, crème de cassis, black cherries, boysenberry, blueberry, and chocolate when young, to fragrances of tobacco, truffle, cedar wood, earth, lead pencil and leather when mature."

Cabernet Sauvignon's popularity as the number one wine in the world can be traced to its propensity for being a stand-alone wine in many regions as well as being used as part of a blend in almost all wine regions.

Again from Jancis Robinson:
> Cabernet Sauvignon has long been planted all over the wine growing world. Contrary to popular belief, Cabernet Sauvignon is not Bordeaux' most planted vine (Merlot is). Because it is relatively late ripening, it needs a warmer, drier environment than most of Bordeaux can provide to stand a commercially interesting chance of ripening fully. In Bordeaux, therefore, it is grown in the Entre-Deux-Mers Region as well as in the well-drained gravels of the Médoc and Graves where it is invariably the chief constituent, but always blended with Merlot, Cabernet Franc and sometimes with Petit Verdot, in the world-famous classed growths. Even today, when the grapes for such wines are being picked later and later, Bordeaux Cabernets tend to taste quite dry (as opposed to sweet) and can be inky and austere even until seven or eight years old. But underpinning all that structure (in a good example) is an extraordinary intensity of subtly layered fruit that can take 20 years to develop into a bouquet of haunting interest.

Food and Cabernet Sauvignon

Steak, steak and more steak! Steaks with a little fat, such as ribeye or a sirloin, but any steak will work, as will a rare burger with cheese. Also with roasted or grilled lamb, and grilled portabella mushrooms.

Cheese: Aged cheddar or Gouda.

Merlot, the Blackbird Wine

The right side of the tasting menu at Wagner Vineyards contains the red wines that we have been discussing. The page starts with a Rosé of Cabernet Franc, followed by Cabernet Franc, then Cabernet Sauvignon, Merlot, Meritage (a Bordeaux blend), and two Pinot Noirs. Tasters are allowed five choices. Despite the fact that the Finger Lakes Region is famed for its world-class white wines, many visitors want only reds. The one red that is most commonly *not* checked is Merlot. You just read that Cabernet Sauvignon is the most popular wine and most planted grape on Earth. As you know, it is a grape from France's Bordeaux Region. But in the Bordeaux and throughout France, *Merlot* is the most planted grape, and the number three most planted grape in the world.

Merlot is a difficult grape to grow in the Finger Lakes because, like most of us, it likes a full day of sun. The sun sets around six pm on the west side of Seneca Lake. Even on the east side, where Wagner Vineyards gets summer sun until after 9 pm, the grape does not always develop enough *brix* to make a good Merlot. (Brix is a measurement of the grapes' sugar content.) People tend not to want to try the Wagner Vineyards Merlot because other Merlots they've tasted on the wine trail have not been good. I will usually "force" our Merlot on them, with very good results.

The other disdain for Merlot comes from the 2004 movie, Sideways. The main character, Miles Raymond (played by Paul Giamatti), did not like Merlot. One of the most memorable lines from the film is Miles colorfully proclaiming his disdain for the wine by saying, "No, if anyone orders Merlot, I'm leaving. I am not drinking any fucking Merlot!" (Apparently Merlot was his ex-wife's favorite wine.) The character much preferred Pinot Noir. (Pinot sales have increased in California over 170% since the movie.) The movie was nominated for five Academy Awards, including Best Picture (it lost to Million Dollar Baby) and is on many "Best Movies of All Time" lists. It was the "most reviewed" movie of 2004 and one of the most popular movies of the year.

Because of the film's popularity, Merlot sales dropped 2%, while Pinot Noir sales increased 16% in the Western United States. These numbers and changes to the wine industry are now called "The Sideways Effect."

A study done fifteen years later found that the movie slowed the growth in Merlot sales and caused its price to fall, but the film's main effect on the wine industry was a rise in the sales volume and price of Pinot Noir, as well as in overall wine consumption. I still believe that some of the unpopularity of Merlot is due to the "hangover" from Sideways.

But, Merlot lovers, fear not! After 15 years, Merlot is making a comeback. The actual decline of Merlot sales began before the movie was released. Famed Napa Valley winemaker, Aaron Pott, who produces under his "Majesty's Secret Service" label and has a vineyard in Napa's Mt. Veeder, actually appreciates the "Sideways effect." In northern California, Pott notes, "It's the best thing that ever happened to Merlot. So much Merlot was being planted back then and it was green (vegetal) and boring. It was being planted in soils that it should never have been planted in. Only the cream went to the top and some good Merlot survived. I remember the quality of Merlot some 15 to 20 years ago. There was a lot of pretty awful Merlot flooding the market."

What Miles stated resonates as true, as many wine-lovers looked down on all that sub-par American Merlot. Today, because of the improved quality of Merlot, sales are on the rise, and many Americans are again calling Merlot their favorite wine.

Of the Bordeaux reds grown in the Finger Lakes, many consider Merlot the most difficult to grow successfully. It does not like the extreme cold of Finger Lakes winters and, as stated above, it seems to enjoy the full day of sun it gets on the west side of Seneca Lake. The clay and shale soils in the Finger Lakes are very similar to the soils in the Bordeaux Region, where Merlot thrives. The warm summer days and cool nights are not only perfect for Riesling, but very suitable for Merlot.

Grapes grow in cone-like clusters. Merlot clusters seem to be looser and therefore easier to pick from its cluster, and the grapes seem to be larger and have a higher sugar content than the two Cabernets. The color of Merlot appears lighter and the skins thinner, which translates to less tannin. Merlot is the first of the Bordeaux grapes harvested, sometimes as long as two weeks before Cabernet Sauvignon. Remember that, when the blackbirds discovered them, the Merlot grapes were already fully ripened and ready, before Franc and Sauvignon.

I will borrow a description of Merlot from Wine Enthusiast Magazine:

> Merlot is known as a chameleon because it adapts to many climates, taking on the character of both its location and winemaking techniques. However, great Merlot is not as easy to grow as people thought, leading to over planting and an abundance of poor quality wines. Typically, Merlot is a dry, medium- to full-bodied wine with moderate acidity, moderate to high alcohol, and soft but present tannin. The best Merlot taste has a range of flavors, ranging from graphite, herbs and blackberries, to black cherries, plums, and cocoa, often layered with notes of clove, vanilla, and cedar when aged in oak.

The article from Wine Enthusiast goes on to compare Merlot with Cabernet and why they are such good blending partners. "Cabernet for its cassis, herbal undertones, and tannin structure and Merlot for its supple texture and ripe fruit. Merlot is usually cheaper, fruitier, and softer than Cabernet, and often perceived as less complex."

Food and Merlot

Grilled chops (veal, pork or lamb), especially with herbs such as thyme and rosemary, steak (especially in a red wine sauce)

Cheeses: Gouda, Gorgonzola, Brie, and Jarlsberg.

Chapter Seven: Pinot Noir, the Elegant Red

In Chapter 5, I chronicled my history of the three Bordeaux reds that we offer at Wagner Vineyards, and how I explain their history to our customers. I did not include Pinot Noir in the narrative because Pinot Noir is not a Bordeaux grape. So, if you continue at my tasting bar, after hearing about the famed grapes from the Bordeaux, I would conclude my presentation of the Wagner Reds with this about my favorite red wine: Pinot Noir.

Famed winemaker, André Tchelistcheff, once declared that "God made Cabernet Sauvignon whereas the Devil made Pinot Noir." He was certainly not talking about the taste of a great Pinot; he was talking about the total process necessary to arrive at that taste.

Cabernet Franc, Sauvignon, and Merot are similar in appearance on the vine, and their individual grapes are easily removed from the clusters. Pinot Noir grapes are much more tightly clustered; you almost have to pry a grape from the cluster. They are so tightly bound that they look like pinecones. In French, "Pinot" means pine cone, and of course, "Noir" means black. The Pinot Noir grape was known as the "Black Pinecone."

Pinot Noir is considered one of the three oldest grapes in the world. (Savagnin, from Chapter 3, and Gouais Blanc, from Chapter 4, are two of the others.) Pinot Noir's DNA has been traced back to well over 2000 years ago. Many historians have surmised that the wine that Jesus created at the Wedding of Cana could have been Pinot Noir.

As already noted in Chapter 4, around 50 BC, the Roman Empire attacked and defeated the Gauls and added France to their growing empire. Also previously mentioned, the Romans had a habit of planting something from their soil (either conquered soil or otherwise) in newly acquired territory. They planted the Pinot Noir grape in what is, today, the Burgundy Region of France.

Go to the French wine section in any large liquor store and you will first see many, many bottles labeled Bordeaux. Look a little further on the shelf and you will also find many bottles of Burgundy. That is Pinot Noir. Burgundy *is* Pinot Noir. (As you learned in Chapter 4, White Burgundy is Chardonnay.) The only place that Pinot Noir can be called Burgundy is in the Burgundy Region of France.

Pinot Noir is the tenth most widely planted grape in the world. It is a very difficult grape to grow, no matter where it is grown, due to its thin skin and susceptibility to disease. The grape does best in cool, dry climates with well drained, chalk laden soils. It is ideally suited to the Finger Lakes, in summers when the Finger Lakes Region is devoid of constant summer rain.

As mentioned, the skin of a Pinot Noir Grape is one of the thinnest in the vineyard. As the Pinot grapes are being punched in the warehouse immediately after harvest, to sit on their skins for a week to develop color and impart tannin to the juice, the thin skins will lend less color and lower levels of tannin than a Bordeaux red. Pinot is, therefore, described as a "light-bodied" red wine.

Pinot is now considered the most popular red wine of its kind in the world. When young, the wine's color is often compared to that of a garnet, as it is frequently much lighter than other red wines. If you *do* see a Pinot that seems darker than most, it has probably been blended with a darker Bordeaux style wine.

The thin skins make the Pinot grape more susceptible to temperature changes while on the vine in the cooler climates where it does best. The tight clusters also make the grape susceptible to diseases such as "bunch rot." **(See Appendix IX)** After reading about my Pinot picking experience in Appendix IX and after reading about the rot that plagues this grape, you can understand Tchelistcheff's statement about the Devil having a hand in the creation of the Pinot grape. Unlike Bordeaux grapes, Pinot does not readily adjust to dramatic changes in vineyard conditions, especially in the cool climate of the Finger Lakes region. Tchelistcheff went on to say that to count the number of great Cabernet Sauvignons that he has made, you would need all your fingers and toes, but to count the number of great Pinots he has created, you would need just one hand, with fingers left over. But then, André's palate was very different from yours and mine.

Wine experts would tell you that a young Pinot can have red fruit aromas of cherries, raspberries, and strawberries. Jancis Robinson adds, "Pinot can vary enormously but its essential characteristic is charm. It tends to be fruity, perfumed and haunting. It dances on the palate rather than overpowering it. High levels of tannin and deep colour are not essential elements in a fine Pinot Noir—not even in a young Pinot Noir. In fact some of my favourite Burgundies are not grand, long-living monsters but lively, sprightly essences of place, sometimes just a general village wine."

Pinot Noir is one of the few red grapes that's commonly made into red, Rosé, white, and sparkling wine. Yes, Pinot Noir is one of the three grapes in a classic Champagne. You may have been wondering about Pinot Gris and Pinot Blanc. DNA analysis has shown that the three Pinots (Noir, Gris, and Blanc) are basically the same grape. The difference is in the colors of the grapes' skin. (Pinot Noir is the classic black/red grape; Pinot Gris, although a white wine grape, normally with a green skin, has a dark grayish skin; and Pinot Blancs have the classic white wine greenish skin.)Thin-skinned grapes tend to lead to clones and mutations. **(See Appendix X)**

As you just read (I hope you have been reading the appendices!), when grapes have similar DNA profiles but look different, they are mutations. Pinot Gris appeared so similar to Pinot Noir that it was originally made into a red wine. But centuries ago, winemakers found that it actually lends itself far better to white wine.

The surge in popularity of Pinot Noir in this country can be directly traced to 2004 and the release of the movie, Sideways. As outlined in Chapter 6, while discussing Merlot, Merlot sales dropped 2%, and Pinot Noir sales rose an astounding 16% nationally. A 2009 study by Sonoma State University found that Sideways slowed the growth in Merlot sales volume and caused its price to fall, but that the film's effect on the wine industry was a rise in the sales volume and price of Pinot Noir and in overall wine consumption. A 2014 study by Vineyard Financial Associates estimated that Sideways cost American Merlot farmers over $400 million in lost revenue in the decade after the movie's release.

Food and Pinot Noir

If the Devil made Pinot Noir, the Devil must have loved to eat, too. The Devil's Pinot is one of the most food-friendly wines in the world. Perfect Pinot Noir pairings include pork (yes, including bacon), beef tenderloin, many cheeses, fish, lamb, mushrooms (sautéed or in a creamy sauce), fresh herbs, and wild game. And don't forget the chocolate! It is a "one wine fits all courses" dinner wine. Tiny spareribs for an appetizer, followed by filet mignon with mushroom sauce, finished with chocolate mousse.

Cheeses: Gouda, Gruyere, Talliggo, light cheddar

Stacy Slinkard, writing for The Spruce Eats, sums it up perfectly:

> Pinot Noir is often described as having a red-wine palate profile and a white-wine style, making it popular with both red-wine and white-wine enthusiasts. Without a doubt, Pinot Noir tends to be lighter bodied than many of its red-wine counterparts (although significant, delicious exceptions do occur) and enjoys a more subtle tannin structure due to the thinner skin of the Pinot Noir grape itself. However, it's the combination of great acidity, silky tannin, and distinct body that makes it so successful for pairing with a tremendous variety of foodie favorites.

Chapter Eight: Sparkling Wine and Wagner Vineyards Sparkling Riesling

British Prime Minister Winston Churchill was an avid consumer of fine Champagne. When addressing his British troops before the invasion of France in June, 1944, he said, "Remember gentlemen, it's not just France we are fighting for, it's Champagne!"

I confess that I am not a huge fan of Champagne or any sparkling wine. My last taste of Tequila was May 29, 1970. My last shot of the French anise-flavored liqueur, Pernod, was July 21, 1979, and my last full glass of Champagne was December 24, 1987. All, of course, are stories of drinking to excess—and a most unpleasant outcome. While tequila and Pernod have not passed my lips since then, I will have an occasional taste of sparkling wine, perhaps once a decade, generally as part of a toast. Given the world's affinity for Champagne, I am most certainly in the minority, but I cannot agree with Mark Twain, who said, "Too much of anything is bad, but too much Champagne is just right."

The monks again, in this case the Benedictine monks, deserve the praise—or blame—for the first sparkling wine. They wrote of sparkling wine in 1531, in their abbey in the medieval city of Carcaassone, in the south of France. It seems that the monks had unintentionally bottled their wine before the fermentation was complete. Almost a century and a half later, the cellar master at the French Abbey of Hautvillers, a Benedictine monk named Dom Pierre Pérignon, discovered the method for creating modern Champagne. But, six years before Pérignon began working with sparkling wine, English scientist Christopher Merret began adding sugar to an existing wine to create a second fermentation, thus creating bubbles (carbon dioxide) and a sparkling wine. He wrote of his findings in 1662, describing his technique, which is now known as méthode champenoise.

Although not the founder of the method (or of Champagne), it was the monk, Pérignon, who pioneered techniques still used today to create

Champagne and sparkling wine. He became an expert in blending various grapes to make a better wine. He perfected the art of taking red grapes and creating white wine. He also perfected a style for his wines to retain their sugar to force a second fermentation. Thicker bottles were created in England to house Pérignon's sparkling wines because the pressure from the developing CO_2 bubbles was too much for the thinner French bottles, many of which exploded!

Pérignon's abbey was in the Champagne Region of France, nestled in the country's northeastern corner, near Paris. This area was originally cultivated by the Romans as early as 400 AD. Today, there are 319 villages in the region and 76,000 acres of vineyards fostering the grapes used to make the iconic sparkling wine.

Over many years, this region produced Europe's finest sparkling wines, called Champagne. The winemakers in this region were so territorial that, by the end of "The Great War," (World War I), the French government began to take steps to prevent other regions from using "Champagne" in naming their sparkling wines. The Treaty of Versailles ended The Great War in 1919. The treaty, which was never signed by the United States, contained a stipulation that signing countries agree not to use the term "Champagne" for their sparkling wines. Today, the European Union forbids any member country and wine region from using "Champagne" in naming a sparkling wine. In 2006, the United States finally banned the use of the term by anyone who had not previously had approval to use it.

"Méthode champenoise" (méthode traditionnelle)

This is the actual method in which the entire fermentation process takes place in the bottle, the steps taken to make Champagne in the Champagne Region of France or elsewhere around the world. In Spain, to produce Cava; in Portugal, to produce Espumante; and in Italy, to produce Franciacorta. Even the use of the term méthod champenoise is limited to members of the European Union. It can only be used in the Champagne Region of France. Elsewhere, it is called "méthode traditionnelle."

The vast majority of Champagnes consist of three grapes, or three previously fermented wines. They are Chardonnay, Pinot Noir and Pinot Meunier (a mutation of Pinot Noir that provides body and richness to Champagne). Other accepted Champagne grapes are Pinot Blanc, Pinot Gris, Petit Meslier, and Arbane. (Petit Meslier is a cross of Gouais Blanc and Savagnin.) We learned that, along with Pinot Noir, Gouais Blanc and Savignin are among the oldest grapes in the world.

Arbane is almost extinct, with less than $2^{1/2}$ acres of it remaining in France. If, after reading previous chapters, you are thinking that Chardonnay, Pinot Meunier, Pinot Blanc and Pinot Gris all have Pinot Noir in their DNA, you would be correct.

Blanc de Blancs (White of Whites) Champagne is made with only white grapes, usually just Chardonnay.

Emily Bell, of Vinepair, writes, "Generally speaking, a Blanc de Blancs will be a bit lighter and dryer, while Blanc de Noirs (Champagne with white and red grapes) will showcase a bit more body and fruity fleshiness. A Blanc de Noirs made entirely from Pinot Noir will have a bit more robustness than one made from a mixture of Pinot Noir and Pinot Meunier. At the end of the day there are many variables beyond grapes that determine what a bottle tastes like. Bottles of 100% Chardonnay Blanc de Blancs from two different producers could taste significantly different (within the context of a bright, dry Champagne, anyway). And then there are producers making Blanc de Blancs without any Chardonnay at all. You're less likely to encounter that, unless you're a big Champagne drinker seeking out new bubbly experiences, so your best bet is to try semi affordable bottles of each and see where your palate feels happiest. It's Champagne, so chances are, all of the above."

The grapes for a sparkling wine are usually harvested early, wanting lower levels of sugar and higher levels of acid. The red grapes are pressed immediately so that the juice remains white. Then the grapes are fermented separately, producing three wines with fairly high acid. The winemakers then decide upon the blend that will be the basis for the sparkling wine. For genuine Champagne, the ratios vary, with about 90% of all blended Champagnes using two-thirds red and one-third Chardonnay mixes. WineCountry.com writes that, "This is based on the structure, fruitiness, body, aroma, delicacy, freshness, and complexity of the grapes. The most commonly used wines for blending Champagne—Chardonnay, Pinot Noir, and Pinot Meunier—are a harmonious combination of all of these revered characteristics."

The blend of the three fermented wines is known as a "cuvée." The cuvée goes into a much heavier, thicker bottle than is used for other wines. Yeast and a small amount of sugar, the "liqueur de tirage," are added to the bottle. (Remember: yeast + sugar = alcohol and carbon dioxide, i.e., bubbles.) A temporary cap, like you might find on a beer or soda bottle, is then applied. (If you look at the neck of an opened bottle of sparkling wine, you can see the lip that held the temporary cap in place.)

After the temporary cap is in place, the bottles are stored on their sides while the second fermentation takes place. For Champagne, if the curvée blend comes from different vintages, as it often does, it is called NV (non-vintage) and must be aged a minimum of 15 months. If the harvest was exceptional and the cuvée was from a single vintage, the wine must age for three years. "Champagne-style" sparkling wine, made in regions and countries outside of the Champagne Region, is not required to follow these rules to the letter. After all, that product is not genuine Champagne.

You have to remember that I was once a teacher (so I repeat myself... over and over and over). The natural sugar in grape juice reacts with the yeast to create alcohol and carbon dioxide. For wine, beer, and whiskey, the CO_2 is vented out. In the Champagne or sparkling wine bottle, the bubbles are trapped, forming pressure, thus requiring the heavier bottle to prevent it from exploding. The amount of sugar added by the winemaker determines the pressure in the bottle, and increases the alcohol content by an average of 1.3%. After the sparkling wine is aged to specification for Champagne (or to the winemaker's desires for non-Champagne sparkling wines), the bottle then goes through a process called "riddling." The "lees" (dead yeast) must be removed from the bottle. So, in stages, the bottles are turned upside down to allow the dead yeast to migrate to the neck of the bottle.

"Disgorging" is next. The upside down bottles are placed in a device that freezes the dead yeast in the neck of the bottle. The temporary cap is then popped and the CO_2 blows out the dead yeast plug. A mixture of the base wine plus sugar, and the preservative sulfur dioxide are then added to the bottle. This mixture is known as the "dosage." The amount of sugar added in the dosage determines the sweetness of the Champagne, and helps to balance the high acid. The bottles are then corked, wired, labeled, and eventually consumed. Consumed by the rich and famous. Consumed by the not-so-rich and famous. Consumed on special occasions and celebrations. "I drink Champagne when I win, to celebrate... and I drink Champagne when I lose, to console myself." (Napoleon Bonaparte)

There are variations of méthode champenoise. Wagner Vineyards uses the "transfer method" for its Sparkling Riesling. This method is identical to the méthode champenoise, except the aged sparkling wines need not be riddled and disgorged in precisely the same manner. Instead, the bottles are emptied into a pressurized tank and sent through pressurized filters to remove the dead yeast. The pressurized wine is then bottled, corked, wired and labeled. Our winemakers feel that this method allows the fruit of the Riesling grape to shine.

Food and Sparkling Riesling
Buttered popcorn (really). Lobster. Caviar. Oysters. Shrimp and other shellfish, smoked salmon, fried calamari. Salami, veggies, stuffed mushrooms, egg dishes, foie gras.

Cheeses: Triple Crème and Marscapone.

Chapter Nine: Rosé

I'm not a big fan of clichés. I have never said, nor will I ever say, "Rosé all day." Perhaps, "Rosé all summer," but, "Rosé all day?" Jamais!

Remember, the juice of almost all red grapes is white. Squeeze any of our Bordeaux grapes (or our Pinot Noir) and you get clear, "white" juice. (The exception is a classification of red grapes known as Teinturier. They include Alicante Bouschet, Chambourein, and Saperavi. The juice of *those* grapes is red.) Whereas *white* grapes are crushed and the juice sent immediately to the fermenters, the *red* grapes are left in the huge bins where they were put immediately after harvesting. The bins hold nearly a ton of freshly harvested grapes. At Wagner Vineyards, the bins are then taken to a warehouse where yeast is added and the winemaking process begins. For the next week, the staff stands on top of the bins, and punches the grapes, with a long pole that has a large flat surface at the end, two to three times a day. At the end of the week, the formerly clear juice is now red from sitting on the dark red to black skins of the grapes. The skins and seeds contain a compound, tannin, which also becomes part of the juice/wine. **(See Appendix VII)**

At Wagner Vineyards, a Rosé of the red Cabernet Franc grape spends only twelve hours on the skins, just long enough for the juice to turn pink.

The Cabernet Franc grape picked for the Wagner Rosé is harvested at midnight in October when the weather is very cool. The harvest is cold-soaked for 12 hours to prevent any wild yeast from starting. This soaking also creates the nice pink color for which Wagner Rosés are known. They have no tannin and never see oak. *It is literally the white wine of a red grape.* A red wine that results from this process (like our Cabernet Franc, Sauvignon, Merlot, or Pinot) is not its natural taste. We manipulate the taste by adding tannin and the taste of oak to the wine by having it sit in an oak barrel. Imagine going into a liquor store to buy a bottle of red wine for a friend's birthday. If you were to see a bottle of white wine labeled Cabernet, Merlot or Pinot, the chances that you'll buy it are somewhere between slim and none. So winemakers leave the juice on the skins for a few hours to turn it pink; then they invent a fancy name like Rosé, and it practically flies off the shelves.

The earliest evidence of winemaking dates back to 6000 years BC Jumping a few thousand years ahead to the ancient Greeks and Romans, we know that winemaking became common throughout the territories conquered and claimed by these ancient civilizations. It was sufficiently important that the Romans made it a habit to cultivate vineyards with roots they imported from other parts of the Roman Empire. It is not really known when the first Rosé wine was intentionally produced, but the earliest of red wines would have appeared more pinkish than red, looking like today's Rosés. Early winemakers pressed red grapes soon after harvest, with very little extended contact between the white juice and the red skins. The result was a pinkish "red" wine with low tannin. The ancients pressed the grapes using their hands and feet (yes, the famed scene from "I Love Lucy!"). The juice produced in this manner was just lightly pigmented. This style of fruitier, pinkish-red wine lasted well into the Middle Ages. British wine writer, Hugh Johnson, considered by many to be the world's foremost wine writer, called the early red wines, "vin d'une nuit" or "wine of one night." These beloved early, pale red wines of the Middle Ages were allowed just one night of contact between juice and skin. The early wine-drinking population considered the darker, redder wines to be much too harsh.

At Wagner Vineyards, we offer a Dry Rosé of Cabernet Franc, as well as two sweet Blush blends. It's easy to tell a curious customer that a Rosé is a *dry* pink wine that spends limited time on the skins and that a Blush is a *sweet* pink wine that is a combination of a sweet white wine and a sweet red wine. We say that in spite of the fact that there are no legal definitions for these terms.

There are Rosés on the market that are a blend of white and red grapes. And there are Blush wines on the market that are a result of leaving the grapes on the skins only briefly. The majority of Blushes seem to be of poor quality and do not age well. They are typically made from inferior hybrid wine and are sweetened to hide their flaws.

Many French winemakers take a different approach to creating a Rosé. In an attempt to create red wines with more tannin and with a deeper color, they remove some of the pink juice from the "must" (the mixture that contains the juice, skins, stems, and seeds— from the Latin vinum mustum, "young wine"), leaving a more concentrated juice to sit on the skins. The French call this the Saignée method. The pink juice is further fermented and becomes Rosé. In France, it is illegal to combine red and white wine unless it is for Champagne. Generally, therefore, a Rosé is a drier wine with limited skin contact, and a Blush is a blend of sweeter white and red wines, but again, since there is no *legal* definition, that is not always the case.

Well after the Middle Ages, and shortly after World War II, two wines from Portugal "caught the world by storm." Lancers and Mateus, two sweet pink wines in somewhat unusual bottles would set sales records in both Europe and the United States. Sales remained strong throughout the 20th Century. And then came White Zinfandel. I borrow the following from Adam Teeter and the Vinepair website:

> *During the 1970s in California, Bob Trinchero and the rest of the team at Sutter Home were trying to create a deeper, more intense Zinfandel. (Zinfandel is a variety of black-skinned wine grape. The variety is grown in over 10 percent of California vineyards). In order to achieve their desired result, they decided to skim off over 500 gallons of the liquid that had only been soaking with the skins for a few short days since the grapes had been pressed. Their thinking was that if they removed some of the liquid, the ratio of more skins to less remaining liquid would create the intense red Zinfandel they were looking for, much like using two tea bags instead of one brews a stronger cup. The issue then became, what the heck to do with the juice they had skimmed off. That juice had become a Rosé, it had a pink color and was very dry, so they decided*

to bottle it and sell it to the public, but fearing consumers wouldn't respond to the name Rosé, they called it White Zinfandel instead. (Basically the Saignée method used in France...) The White Zinfandel sold well for the first few years Sutter Home made it, but it didn't truly become a phenomenon until another accident turned the wine into the sweet liquid we now know it as. In 1975, while Sutter Home was making their White Zinfandel, they experienced a Stuck Fermentation, which basically means the yeast all die before they're through converting all the sugar to alcohol. The result was a wine that was boozy to be sure, but still had some sugar left behind, making it sweet. The wine was a massive success, no doubt driven by its drinkability and cheap price tag, and Sutter Home became the champion of the movement, creating the cheap, sweet wine in massive quantities.

Unfortunately, the low price, combined with White Zinfandel's sweetness, ultimately became its undoing. As more people became wine drinkers, they were exposed to well-made dry Rosés from places like France (and Wagner Vineyards). Those wines were refreshing, crisp, and perfect with food, and the sweet pink wine would no longer do.

Currently, White Zinfandel is making a comeback, though not led by the folks at Sutter Home, who are still making the wine the same way they have for decades. Instead, young winemakers in California are playing with America's new-found love for Rosé and aversion to White Zinfandel by creating dry Rosés from the Zinfandel grape and, of course, calling them White Zin.

So the next time you think you love Rosé but hate White Zinfandel or vice versa, remember it's the *style* of the wine you don't like, either dry or sweet, because in terms of how they're made, they are identical, except that the sweetness of White Zin, which most Rosés lack, came from a happy accident. Happy for the people at Sutter Home, but not so "happy" for a dry wine drinker.

Let's put "pink pieces" together. To put the name of a grape on a bottle of wine, ie., Chardonnay, Riesling, Pinot Noir, 75% of the wine in the bottle must be from that grape. That is a law in the United States. There are, however, no such laws about using the terms Rosé or Blush on a bottle. Could a blend of a dry Riesling and a Pinot Noir be called a Blush or a Rosé? Yes, it could. Could a wine that spent only limited time on the skins also be called either Blush or Rosé? Again, yes. Taking White Zinfandel out of the equation, can you generally call a dry pink wine left on the skins for a short amount of time a Rosé? Yes, you can. If you blend together a sweet white and a sweet red, can you call it a Blush? Yes, you can.

Food and Rosé

Light Salads (Greek Salad). Light Pasta. Seafood & cooked Shellfish. Melon, prosciutto, anchovies.

Cheese: Goat Cheese.

Chapter Ten: Ice Wine

When I think of ice, I think cold: Ice skating, icebergs, ice cream, Siberia, snow, igloos, a cold night, a cold drink, and a cold climate. Ice wine can be produced only in cold climates. The Finger Lakes Region certainly meets that requirement.

I remember the winter of 2014-15, when not one minute of February was above freezing, when pipes froze (and subsequently burst). And I remember many nights where the temperature dropped to -20° or below. Fortunately for residents, while every winter in the Finger Lakes is cold, they aren't typically quite as cold as that winter was. It is, however, always cold enough to create ice wine.

To make Ice Wine, the grapes must be frozen *on the vine*. When the grapes and the water inside them freeze, the sugars and dissolved solids do not. The result is an extremely concentrated and sugary liquid that emerges when the grapes are ultimately pressed. The frozen grapes are not normally affected by the scourge of noble rot; they are incredibly sweet with high acid. A "sweet wine" will hover between 5 and 7 percent residual sugar. **(See Appendix XI)** The residual sugar of ice wine can approach 20% or more. *That* is sweet.

The whole process from harvest to press takes about six hours, and can only be undertaken when weather conditions are right. Because of this, it can be risky in some years, when the grapes may not freeze at all, and a whole vineyard set aside for ice wine can be lost. In many cases the harvest might not happen until after the new year. Ice Wine is the "pain in the ass" wine. When the weather forecasts a temperature drop to 20°F., you (the winemaker/vineyard master) gather workers. You appeal to your Facebook followers to gather at a time of darkness in the earliest of morning hours. You stand in the cold, often in snow, to hand-pick the grapes, which are immediately pressed. The press is crushing grapes that resemble marbles. The juice is then separated from the seeds and stems before fermentation begins. It may take months to complete the fermentation process because of the grapes' high sugar levels.

It's believed that in Franken, Germany, during a particularly cold winter in 1794, winemakers were forced to create a product from the only grapes available for harvest. The resulting wines from that vintage had an amazingly high sugar content, along with great flavor. Thus, the technique became popular in Germany. By the mid-1800s, the Rheingau Region was making what the Germans called "eiswein."

Even knowing all this about ice wine, actually making it is still a "crap shoot." You are not guaranteed that the temperature will drop to 20°F. You are not guaranteed that the grapes will not simply drop off the vine before they can be harvested. You are not guaranteed that little critters in the vineyards will not eat all of the shriveled grapes. There is an alternative: cryoextraction. No, it's not like freezing someone into suspended animation. Cryoextraction is a special way of preparing grapes for wine making. It is a controlled process that involves freezing the grapes. The grapes are harvested, cleaned and placed in a freezer set to 20°F. Just as with grapes that have frozen on the vine, the grapes in the freezer are removed and placed in a wine press. This produces the highest level of concentrated flavor in the juice from the frozen grapes.

With cryoextraction, it is important that the grapes are at their ripest. Perfectly ripe grapes have a higher sugar content and will freeze more quickly than grapes that are not thoroughly ripened for winemaking. The juice from the frozen grapes will have a greater concentration of sweetness as well as flavor.

To distinguish between the two methods, the government designates that only wine created from grapes frozen while on-the-vine may be called "Ice Wine," while wine made from grapes that were frozen, in a freezer, at harvest must be called "*Iced* Wine."

Although in theory you can make an ice wine from any grape, grapes typically used for Ice Wine include Riesling, considered by German winemakers to be the noblest variety; Vidal Blanc, which is popular in Ontario, Canada; and Cabernet Franc. Some producers are experimenting with other grapes, including Chenin Blanc, Grüner Veltliner, Gewürztraminer, and Merlot. Ice Wines made from white grapes are usually pale yellow or light gold in color when they are young and deepen with age, or pink when made with red grapes.

I have not mentioned price with any of the wines I've described. A "pain in the ass" wine, with all of the extra work, commands a higher price. Ice wines are expensive to make, even when you freeze the grapes yourself. Ice wine requires 4-5 times as many grapes. (A typical bottle of wine averages 750 grapes. An Ice Wine can have over 1,500 grapes!) In addition, they're all hand-picked if made with grapes frozen on the vine. Most Ice Wine comes bottled in the smaller 375 ml bottle (half the size of a typical bottle of wine). Many traditional (handpicked) Ice Wines can cost $50 or more per bottle (or the equivalent of $100 for a 750 ml bottle). If you see ice wines for less, they're probably made with commercially frozen grapes ("*Iced* Wine" or "Riesling Ice") as we do at Wagner Vineyards.

Ice Wine is one of those wines we love to hate. After all, it's almost twice as sweet as Pepsi-Cola. Still, it's hard to despise the wonderful gift created by the combination of grapes and a cold climate. You may have gathered from previous chapters that I am not a fan of sweet wines. I do, on occasion, find a use for dessert wines. Let's say that I prepare your dinner. We start with a shrimp cocktail with heavy horseradish sauce. Your Caesar salad adds anchovies and garlic. We follow with a charred porterhouse with a mushroom stout beer sauce and roasted garlic mashed potatoes, and roasted onions, peppers, zucchini, and eggplant seasoned with basil, oregano, and rosemary. You are too full for the chocolate Pots de Crème, but you say, "Johnny, I have anchovies, garlic, horseradish, onions, peppers, beer sauce and basil, oregano and rosemary on my breath! Please, I need something sweet!" The answer is a small—*very small*—glass of Wagner Vineyards Riesling Ice or Vidal Ice.

Food and Dessert Wine

As Ice Wine is a dessert wine with explosive fruit flavors and on the high-sweetness end of the spectrum, you'll want to pair it with somewhat subtle desserts containing enough fat to balance the taste profile. If you prefer more savory, late-night snacks, a great pairing option with Ice Wine would be softer cheeses.

Non-dessert items that pair well with the ultra-sweet ice wines include nuts, anchovy-infused dishes, foie gras, and pâté. Grilled eel (try it, you'll like it!), fatty fish, and sashimi are other options.

Desserts include custard tarts (chocolate pots de crème), crème brûlée, cheesecake, ice cream, fresh fruit, panna cotta. Also cold melon soups and stone fruits (peaches, nectarines.)

Cheese: Aged cheddar, Brie, Mascarpone.

Chapter Eleven: Blended Wines (Meritage & Fathom 107)

The earliest evidence of wine can be traced to the far Eastern European country of Georgia, formerly part of the USSR. It is bordered to the north by Russia and by Turkey on the south. The evidence dates back to around 6000 BC, approximately 8000 years ago! Remnants of an actual winery were found in Armenia in 2007. Archaeologists dated that winery to 4100 BC, more than 6100 years ago. Excavations uncovered fermentation vats, a wine press, and storage jars. More-modern vineyards, from the days of the Roman conquest, have contained multiple grape types which would be harvested together and made into wine. Though not a true or "modern" blend, it *is* a blend of grapes to make a wine. The Romans vanquished the Gauls and added France to their empire around 50 BC. We have seen how the Romans brought and planted grapes, establishing vineyards as they conquered vast sections of Europe.

The first known or recorded vineyards date back to 71 AD. Much of this wine was consumed by the Roman soldiers. It is almost certain that actual blending of fermented grapes took place at this time. We have learned about the development of Cabernet Franc, Sauvignon, and Merlot in the early 1600s through the late 1700s, and the blending of wines in the Bordeaux Region that dates to the Middle Ages.

The Bordeaux is certainly not the warmest region of France. Early spring rains, chilly nights, and variable weather patterns can make it difficult to grow red grapes. That will sound familiar if you live in the Finger Lakes Region of Central NY.

With the exception of grapes destined for Ice Wine, Cabernet Sauvignon is always the last grape harvested. If the autumn has been cool and frost is predicted, this grape might be harvested before it is ready. The resulting juice will have more acid and higher levels of tannin than a fully ripe Sauvignon. Cabernet Franc and Merlot are sometimes picked several weeks before Cabernet Sauvignon, and can reach full maturity with less heat and sun. Blending the matured Franc and Merlot with the not-quite-ready Sauvignon can create a wonderful wine, and no grapes or juice are wasted. On the flip side, blending fully ripe Cabernet Sauvignon with less-ripe Merlot both tempers the high alcohol of Cabernet and makes Merlot taste fruitier. In great growing seasons the blends can be world class, while in less-than-favorable seasons, good and certainly palatable wines can be produced.

In 2017, Laura Burgess of Vinepair, wrote that, "unlike much of what goes on in today's wine industry, blends weren't the result of a fad, a catchy PR campaign, a TV show, or a Top 40 song. The tradition of blending dates back millennia, to times when mixed vineyards served as an insurance policy against Mother Nature's wrath, and a reliable harvest won out over nuances of flavor.

Like a band of superheroes bonded together for the common good of mankind, a good blend can bring out the extraordinary qualities of ordinary grape varieties. Today, winemakers build blends by layering the unique attributes of different grapes, like color from Petit Verdot, spicy aromas from Cabernet Franc, or plummy notes from Merlot. It's what makes modern wines balanced and hard to put down. Like X-Men or the Fantastic Four, the combined qualities of a blended wine are stronger (a.k.a. more delicious) together than the flavors or aromas of any single grape variety.

Despite the flavor-centric approach to blending that exists today, the history of blended wines has little to do with flavor. In fact, the practice of blending specific grape varieties for their flavor and aromatic qualities didn't become popular until the 1800s, centuries after wine consumption, and even connoisseurship, became fashionable. Historically, a desire for reliability, or for having wine every season, inspired the blend, especially the Bordeaux blends that are now replicated worldwide. Like having the Fantastic Four on retainer, planting a blend of grapes acted as an early insurance policy for farmers against destruction by pests, war, or bad weather.

Wagner Vineyards creates two blended wines: Meritage, a Bordeaux style blend, and Fathom 107, a very interesting blend of the diverse tastes from the Riesling and Gewürztraminer grapes.

Meritage

I mentioned earlier that there are approximately 6000 wineries in the Bordeaux Region of France and, as far as I know, all of them blend their grapes to make a wine that is bottled as a Bordeaux Wine. If you go into the red wine or French section of a liquor store, you will see bottles labeled Bordeaux (or Cru Bourgeois) and you now know that they are a blend of mostly Merlot and Cabernet Sauvignon, with a little Cabernet Franc, and quite possibly some Malbec or Petit Verdot, or very rarely some Carménère. The words/terms Champagne, Bordeaux, and Burgundy are off-limits for use on bottles in the US, as stipulated by the European Union's Protected Designation of Origin. Thus, for years, if Bordeaux blends were created (mostly in California), they were labeled as "red table wine" and possibly named after someone's grandmother.

In 1988, a group of Napa Valley and Sonoma County winery owners held a contest to determine a proprietary name for a wine that blends grapes from the Bordeaux. Six thousand entries were submitted. The winning entry in the contest was "Meritage." The woman who submitted it wrote: "Merit" for the quality of wine in the bottle--just grapes from the Bordeaux--and "Heritage" for the longstanding tradition of blending Bordeaux grapes The correct pronunciation rhymes with the word "heritage." It does *not*, as most people assume, end with the "age" sound of the word "garage." It is also not French. It is very American, but it is too often mispronounced by many who call themselves wine experts.

The Meritage Association was formed in 1988. Although there are no Meritage Police, the stipulation for putting "Meritage" on the label of a bottle of wine is that you must use at least 2 of the Bordeaux grapes listed (plus two other Bordeaux grapes: Saint-Macaire and Gros

Verdot). The blend must not consist of more than 90% of a single grape, and you must promise to make it when all of your grapes blend to create a high quality wine.

To join the Meritage Association you are required to pay one dollar per case, capped at $500. They ask that you not to produce more than 25,000 cases per year.

The first wine to be labeled "Meritage" was the 1986 "The Poet" by Mitch Cosentino (Cosentino Winery). The 1985 vintage by Dry Creek Vineyard was the oldest vintage released "Meritage". (Remember the "vintage" designation is the year in which the grapes were harvested, not the year they were bottled.) The winner of the wine-naming contest received two bottles of the first ten vintages of each wine licensed to use the brand name, Meritage.

In 2009, the Meritage Association became the Meritage Alliance. Today, there are over 350 members, dominated by the US, but with member wineries in Argentina, Australia, Canada, France, Israel and Mexico.

The first Meritage at Wagner Vineyards was produced in 1998. Later bottlings were done in 1999, 2001, 2007, 2010, 2012, and 2016. All were very hot, dry summers. The 2016, released in March of 2020, was awarded 90 points by Wine Advocate Magazine. Mark Squires of Wine Advocate wrote that the Wagner Meritage has a "full-bodied demeanor, impeccable balance and just enough structure to age well for another decade, or more." Not bad for a New York red!

Food and Meritage
Meritage pairs well with savory red meats, either grilled or roasted, including beef, lamb, wild game, veal, and pork. It also pairs with cheese-based pastas and risotto. And chocolate, of course.

Cheeses: Mild and medium sharp cheddar, Edam, Muenster, Smoked Gouda

Fathom 107

Nearly all of the 140 wineries in the Finger Lakes have Rieslings and a Gewürztraminer. And almost none of the region's wineries blend these two grapes. There may be only five blends of these two Vinifera grapes produced in the Finger Lakes, though these grapes flourish in the region's cool climate. Riesling is not only very fruity, but is also extremely acidic. Gewürztraminer is very low in acid, and is known for its floral and spicy finish. Diverse characteristics, yes, and winemakers do not like fooling with the blending of them. Wagner Vineyards not only fools with blending Riesling and Gewürztraminer, but fools with them very well. (This unbiased writer thinks that it is the best white blend in the region.)

Once created, we needed a name for the blend. Winemakers and winery owners tend to name their blends after their mothers and grandmothers or their dead dogs and their favorite cars. We named ours Fathom 107. Of the 123,657 lakes in the United States, 7,612 are in New York State. Seneca Lake, the largest of the Finger Lakes, is the 15th deepest lake in the country. The deepest part of Seneca Lake commands the view from the windows of the Wagner Vineyards Octagon Tasting Room. It is 640' deep. In nautical terms, 640' equals 107 Fathoms. (A Fathom is 6 feet.) When I first heard this story more than four years ago, I looked up a fathom to see if it was part of a "league" (as in the Jules Verne story, "20,000 Leagues Under the Sea"), or if a league was part of a fathom. As I learned, one league equals 3,038 fathoms, so Verne's 20,000 Leagues equals 69,046 miles. That's almost one-third of the distance from Earth to the Moon, proving that Wells' storytelling ability was vastly superior to his math skills!

We have established that the Wagner Vineyards white blend of Riesling and Gewürztraminer is a unique wine. Before I pour this wine for our customers, I always make sure that they taste our dry Riesling and our dry Gewürztraminer. We talk about the stark differences between the two wines. Then I pour the Fathom 107 and tell them to take three or four short sips and try to separate fruit, flowers, and spice. Each taste is a bit different as the brain—yours—tries to separate the various tastes.

It is one of favorite wines at Wagner's and, as I wrote, I think one of the very best white blends in the Finger Lakes.

Food and Fathom 107

Like Gewürztraminer, Fathom 107 generally benefits from dishes with more than a bit of spice.

Cheese: Muenster and soft cow milk cheeses.

Chapter Twelve: The Bottles & the Caps

Now that we've completed the discussion of the award winning wines that I pour at Wagner Vineyards, I thought it would be interesting to discuss the types of bottles and bottle closures that we use for each of the wines. I'm sure that you have noticed that not all wine bottles are alike. There is a history behind the bottles that we use. Bottle shape is pretty consistent among Finger Lakes wineries. When I was in Texas a few years ago, attending the 31st Annual GrapeFest at Grapevine, Texas, I noticed that many of *their* wineries use the same shape bottle for every type of wine they produce. Keep this in mind: *The shape of the bottle has absolutely no impact on the taste or flavor of wine.*

There are hundreds of different bottle shapes, but most classic winemakers tend to use one of these three for their Vinifera wines: the Burgundy bottle, the Bordeaux bottle and the Alsace/Mosel bottle.

The classic Burgundy bottle dates to the 19th Century. It is thought that the curve-sided bottle was chosen because it was the easiest for a bottle maker to create. It is believed that the Burgundy Region was the first to have a uniform bottle to represent an entire region. From previous chapters, you will remember that the region is famous for two great wines: Pinot Noir, the most popular light-bodied red wine in the world, and Chardonnay, the most popular white wine in the world. You also remember that in the Burgundy Region these two wines are known as Burgundy and White Burgundy. Now you also know why they share the same bottle type and design.

Wagner Vineyards uses the classic Burgundy bottle to house its Pinot Noir and Chardonnay wines.

At Wagner Vineyards, the familiar Bordeaux bottle is used for Cabernet Franc, Cabernet Sauvignon, Merlot and Meritage.

Around the time the bottles from Burgundy were created, the first Bordeaux bottle was blown. The bottle's shoulders are more distinctive, leading many to theorize that the high shoulders were formed to catch the sediment when the bottle is decanted. Other "experts" believe that the high, more distinctive shoulders were formed simply to distinguish the bottle and its wine from the Bordeaux cousin in the Burgundy Region.

The Alsace/Mosel bottle, the last of the three "great" wine bottles, was created shortly after the Bordeaux bottle. It was intended to house the up-and-coming Rieslings for the Alsace Region of France and the Mosel of Germany. Later, the makers of Gewürztraminer would also use this bottle. The tall, thin style is far more delicate than its Bordeaux and Burgundy counterparts. The thought behind the taller design was to accommodate the smaller-than-ocean-going vessels that transported the Rieslings and Gewürztraminers along the Rhine River. These small river ships needed to pack as many bottles as possible in the hull of the ship. River travel was much more gentle than ocean travel, thus the bottle could be more delicate.

Wagner Vineyards uses the Alsace/ Mosel bottle for its Gewürztraminer, Riesling and Fathom 107 wines.

The traditional Champagne style bottle is used for Wagner's Sparkling Riesling.

Champagne bottles are similar in shape to those of Burgundy, but they are much thicker and heavier.

As previously explained, the thick glass serves a very important purpose. Champagne is the only wine that is carbonated; the pressure from that carbonation is equal to five times the normal atmospheric pressure.

All of that wine and carbon dioxide—as much as 90 pounds per cubic inch, or 3 times the air pressure in a car tire—demands the thicker glass. If left to fly on its own, a Champagne cork can reach speeds of 30 miles per hour.

Champagne wine bottles are almost always dark green in color. At Wagner Vineyards, the Sparkling Riesling is housed in such a bottle.

The Color of Wine Bottles

Winemakers have been using colored wine bottles since the early 1700s. The most common wine bottle colors are dark green and amber. Other variations include blue, deep brown and frosted. Traditionally, colored wine bottles have been used to limit exposure to light. Sunlight, and even incandescent light, can cause wine to break down, affecting color, aroma, and taste, eventually leading to oxidation. If you remember from science class, oxidation is the process that causes metal to rust. A little bit of oxygen is good for a wine, because it allows the flavors to open up, which is why we decant certain wines. People often refer to this process as "allowing the wine to breathe." However, when a wine has too much contact with oxygen, it starts to get dull. A wine that has been oxidized loses its depth of flavor and can begin to take on a vinegary taste.

The good news is that wines contain natural antioxidants that discourage excessive oxidation from occurring. However, sunlight can often break down both a wine's antioxidants and its tannin. If these substances are weakened, they can't do their job of protecting the wine. Tinted glass blocks this sunlight, preserving the antioxidants and allowing them to protect the wine from oxidation as it ages. While red Bordeaux wines are typically kept in dark green bottles, dry white Bordeaux is kept in lighter green ones. Burgundies, along with Mosels, Alsaces, and plenty of Champagnes, are also kept in green bottles.

Due to better harvesting and fermentation methods, most fine wines don't require extensive aging to acquire peak quality. And, with today's hectic, live-in-the-moment pace, wine is often enjoyed soon after purchase, rather than being stored for months (or years). In fact, it is estimated that 70-90% of wine in the United States is consumed within 24 hours of purchase!

"Punt"

No, it's not the fourth down, but it is fast approaching. There is, of course, a bottom to all of these bottles. It is called the "punt." When these bottles were individually blown by glassblowers in the 1600s, the long device (usually 4 to 6 feet) on which the bottles were blown was called a pontil. It was attached to what would become the bottom of the bottle. A rough edge or "scar" forms where the pontil is attached to the bottom of the finished bottle. Without the familiar indentation on the bottom of the bottle, the scar could cause the bottle to wobble and scratch the surface on which it is set. With modern bottle-making, the traditional punt is no longer actually necessary, but winemakers are traditionalists; they seem to be emotionally attached to the indented punt in their bottles. Before advanced filtering methods were developed, winemakers found that the deep punts in the bottles allowed the sediment in wines to settle and remain around the cone that is formed inside the bottle by the punt.

Modern bottle sizes are:
Piccolo (also called Pony, Snipe or Split), a quarter-bottle, 187 ml.
Demi, a half-bottle, 375 ml.
Standard, 750 ml.
Magnum, a double bottle, 1500 ml.
Jeroboam, a double magnum, 3000 ml.

Because these bottles are typically stored on their sides, in racks, the wine comes into contact with the cork, creating an ideal, oxygen-free seal. This seal protects the wine from oxidation.

Corks and Caps

Those of us who work at a winery, as well as the multitudes who enjoy a great bottle of wine, are accustomed to that familiar, satisfying popping sound of a cork being removed from a newly opened bottle of wine. In recent years, however, the major wine-producing countries of Australia, New Zealand, and many others have moved away from cork. It's time for us to look at cork's history and evolution.

Actual cork usage dates back thousands of years. Corks were used by ancient fisherman to hold up their nets. Conquering Greeks and Romans used cork in their sandals. Cork has even been found in ancient Egyptian tombs. Cork usage in wine bottles did not begin until the late 1600s and early 1700s. As glassblowing became more advanced and the fabricators were able to make thinner necks, corks could be used to seal the wine. (The first easy-to-use corkscrew wasn't invented until the late 1700s.) Before cork, cloth, leather, glass, clay, and sealing wax were used to close wine bottles. Before long, consumers noticed that wine aged with a cork in a now-airtight sealed bottle was better. Wine had entered the "modern age," where it could age and improve in the bottle.

If you visit Spain, Portugal, Algeria, Morocco, France, Italy, or Tunisia, you will find "cork forests." Those "forests" contain evergreen oak trees, Quercus suber. These trees grow to 60' high and 12' across. They are the primary source for the corks used in wine bottles and for other products. This species of tree is more than 60 million years old. The cork comes from the bark of these trees. Once planted, it takes at least 20 years before the bark is ready to be stripped or "harvested" from the tree for cork production. It takes 10 years before cork can be harvested again. These trees, which usually live for 200 years, cover more than five million acres in the world, with more than half of that acreage in Spain and Portugal.

After the bark is stripped from the trees in large planks, it must be dried. It is then boiled to clean, soften, and most importantly, disinfect the cork. This is an essential process for cork that will be used for wine bottles. Finished corks are then sorted and labeled, from top grade to lower grade. Then the corks are boiled *again* to ensure sterilization. (Some are even coated with a very thin coat of wax to guarantee that the cork will not affect the taste of the wine.) These 100% corks are referred to as "Natural" or "Traditional" corks.

Despite all the precautions and sterilization, natural cork can still cause "cork taint." A bottle is deemed "*corked*" if, upon opening and at its highest levels, the wine smells moldy or musty, like cardboard, damp cement or wet newspapers. This renders the wine undrinkable. At lower levels, the taint merely strips a wine of its flavor, making normally rich, fruity wines taste dull or muted, though without a noticeable defect. This can leave consumers disappointed in a wine without being able to pinpoint why. With natural corks, "corked" wine can affect as many as one bottle in every two cases.

Because of the prevalence of "corked" wine, many wineries have turned to agglomerated corks. According to a 2018 blog post from TheAlcoholProfessor.com:

> Despite all the wine closure options out there, traditional cork remains "king" in most markets, with many consumers associating natural cork with wine quality (save for Australia and New Zealand, who prefer the screw cap). In recent years, however, technological corks have been making headway, with these closures increasing in market share in recent years.
>
> One type of technological cork that has seen their market share skyrocket in recent years is the Diam cork. Made using traditional cork, Diam seeks to eliminate the issue of cork taint and provide winemakers with a high level of consistency in aging from year to year, all while maintaining all the traditions of a natural cork.
>
> First, Diam purchases raw cork straight from the producers, breaks it down into tiny particles, and runs it through their patented cleaning process, the Diamant® supercritical CO_2 cleaning technology that was developed exclusively as a cork purification process. Originally developed in the 1950s by Maxwell House to decaffeinate coffee, the Diamant® supercritical CO_2 patent further developed the technology specifically for corks, an industry first.
>
> At a certain temperature and pressure, CO_2 lives in this state between liquid and gas, called the 'supercritical' state. When CO_2 is in this supercritical state, it can penetrate deep into cork and remove the TCA compounds responsible for cork taint, as well as other compounds that may negatively influence the wine.

*After a sifting process to remove any dust or wood
particles, the cork particles then undergo the Diamant®
supercritical CO_2 cleaning process. After cleaning, the
TCA-free cork particles are put back together using
another patented technology that uses food-grade binding
agents and food-grade microspheres, both of which have
been specially notified by the FDA, to provide elasticity
and consistency in the finished corks.*

*In addition to eliminating the issue of cork taint and
promoting consistent aging in every cork, Diam also places
a strong focus on sustainability.*

Wagner Vineyards uses only Diam corks for their red wines, oaked
Chardonnays, and Ice Wines.

When a modern bottling machine is used, a high quality cork will
allow very small amounts of oxygen—perhaps 1 milligram per year of
aging—to infiltrate the bottle. Too much air will cause the wine to
oxidize and lose its fruit character, making it taste bitter. The school
of thought for generations has been that very small amounts of
oxygen, introduced slowly with quality corks, will allow a wine to
mature and the tannin to soften.

As previously mentioned, Australia and New Zealand have moved away
from cork to alternative wine closures. They now use, almost
exclusively for both red and white wines, screw caps or "stelvins." In
the 1970s, shoes with cork heals were all the rage, and cork was
diverted to shoe manufacture—and away from wine corks. With a
shortage of quality cork, wine cork manufacturers sent their highest
grade corks to European winemakers, and the lower quality corks to
Australia and New Zealand. Cork taint became the norm in those two
huge wine producing countries. Wine summits were held, and, by the
turn of the century, both countries were exclusively using screw caps.

In 2001, scientists from the Australian Wine Research Institute
published preliminary results following 20 months of an ongoing study.

They concluded that wine in bottles closed with screw caps remained consistent in taste, unlike the same wines sealed with corks. ***Screw caps provide a seal that is better than that of cork!***

The debate had shifted onto new ground. Now, the key question was whether a seal that is tighter than that provided by cork is actually desirable, and whether red wine in particular *needs* the very small amount of oxygen infiltration permitted by the average cork for successful aging to occur.

New Zealand's Michael Brajkovich was his country's leading advocate of screw caps. As an early adopter, he switched the entire production of his Kumeu River Wines to this closure in 2001. For two years, he was chairman of the NZ Screw Cap Wine Seal Initiative, and is still on the committee. In 2003, he talked about oxygen transfer for aging red wines.

> *The answer is twofold. Firstly, it's very difficult to measure. We are talking about incredibly tiny amounts of gas transmission. Secondly, and more importantly, wine aging is a complicated chemical process that is poorly understood. It's not possible to determine the effect of tiny amounts of extraneous oxygen over many decades other than by just seeing what happens with a real wine. It's a frustrating situation. Now that it's possible to dial up or down the amount of oxygen transfer that a screw cap allows, by toying with the wadding composition, if we knew that the oxygen transfer level allowed by an average cork were ideal for red wine development, then we could produce screw caps that sealed to a similar degree, but which would offer much greater consistency and the absence of taint. I suspect that it will turn out that a very low oxygen transmission rate, similar to that with a normal screw cap, will be the most desirable for bottle ageing. This would support the notion that bottle maturation is a chemically reductive process that takes place despite the ingress of oxygen, not because of it.*

I remember $1 bottles of wine in the late '60s and '70s, when the drinking age was 18. Boone's Farm, Thunderbird and Wild Irish Rose had screw caps, signaling very cheap wine. Wagner Vineyards and other quality winemakers have recently gone from cork closures for their white wines to stelvins. (Stelvin is a brand name for a screw cap, but they are so prevalent in the industry that all screw caps are called stelvins. It's like asking for a "xerox" when you want a copy, or a "kleenex" when you want to blow your nose, or "scotch" tape if you want to wrap a gift.)

The American wine consuming public is slowly coming to understand that a screw cap on a white wine no longer signals that it is a cheap wine.

Stelvins consist of a metal cap with a liner inside the top of the cap that attaches to the bottle lip for its seal. Screw caps consist of two components. First, there is the cap itself, which comes attached to the sleeve. This is made of an aluminum alloy. Second, we have the business end of the screw cap—the liner—which is made of an expanded polyethylene wadding. This is typically covered with a tin foil layer that acts as a barrier to gas exchange. In theory, these caps prevent air from entering the bottle. Since corks are porous and allow very small amounts of oxygen to slowly enter the bottle, the prevailing theory is that this small amount of oxygen allows the wine to age and evolve, improving over years of storage in your wine cellar. Some screw cap manufacturers now construct their stelvins to allow limited amounts of oxygen to enter the bottle, thus mimicking the beneficial effect of natural cork.

The use of screw caps eliminates any chance of cork taint and over-oxidation. They are also much easier to open, and much, much easier to reseal.

Experts are experts—even though they do not necessarily agree. Someone writes a paper or a book, creates something new or recreates something old, and is called an expert. The experts do not agree on whether it is beneficial or desirable to allow tiny amounts of oxygen to infiltrate a bottle of wine. There are some who contend that modern corks are so good that air cannot enter. Many write that the small amount of oxygen that enters each bottle every year softens the tannin and matures the wine. Still other experts argue that the small amount of oxygen entering a bottle when it is bottled is enough to soften the tannin over time.

White wine has no tannin to soften. It is also a fact that most white wines do not age as well as red wines. Wagner Vineyards and other wineries have gone to stelvins for only their white wines. In conducting their own tests, the wine making team at Wagner's concluded that, over time, a white wine retains its original character longer when closed with a stelvin than when sealed with a cork. As seen throughout this discussion, the jury is still out when it comes to the aging of red wine. Time will tell.

CONCLUSION

We have learned (I hope) that not all people taste the same wine the same way. Big words and mentions of fruit or wet stones are not going to enhance a wine for you. You taste a wine, you think about it, and you either smile...or you do not. You think, "I can drink this," or you know that you cannot. If you are at a dinner table or at a friend's house and it is the only bottle available, then you have decisions to make. If you are standing in front of me, tasting Wagner Vineyards wines, your decisions can be a lot easier.

I have given you the history of the grape, perhaps its DNA breakdown, and theories about how it got to the area(s) of Europe where it became famous. None of that had anything to do with you deciding that you want more of that wine.

Two kinds of customers frequent our tasting bars—those who come in with the intention of buying wine, and those who do not. There are many "tasters" who do just that: they taste. They enjoy the experience and then they move to the next stop on the wine trail. They are not the wine buyers. Other visitors travel along the wine trail to fill their wine libraries with the wines that they found to be impressive. I treat everyone as if they are wine buyers. After all, I can sometimes convert a "taster" to a buyer.

I have never been a follower. I have always taken my own road or carved out a road where one did not exist. I took a different approach to pouring wine, as described in the preceding pages. Since Konstantin Frank opened his "Vinifera Winery" in the early 1960s, New York's Finger Lakes Region has become the center of New York's Vinifera production. After the Farm Winery Act of 1976, pioneers like Bill Wagner followed Dr. Frank to build a wine region that is now recognized the world over. The award-winning wines at Wagner's have made my job most enjoyable. (I don't really think of it as "work") At 72, I still love to work. I have been fortunate to have always enjoyed what I have done. I enjoy coming to work each day. Writing about what I do was easy—time consuming, but easy.

Life is full of choices. If every Riesling or Chardonnay or Merlot at every winery tasted the same, there would be no need for a wine trail. You have many choices in buying a car, in choosing a laundry detergent, or in taking your significant other to a restaurant. As I have mentioned throughout this book, I am very fortunate to be teaching about and pouring some of the very finest wines in the Finger Lakes Region. There are many choices to be made here. In many cases, the choices are, "How many different wines should I buy?" or "How many bottles should I purchase?" Connecting with people, or more specifically, connecting with "wine" people, and teaching about the wines without telling everyone how and what they are tasting is what inspired me to write this book.

I hope that the "window" was clear and that your view was enjoyable!

The Looking at Wine Through a Different Window: THE COOKBOOK

In the book that I hope you just finished reading, I discussed the "Noble Wines" that I proudly pour every day at Wagner Vineyards. At the end of the discussion of each wine, I listed various foods that could be enjoyed with wine, including cheeses that could—and should—be served with the wine. When discussing Riesling, Gewürztraminer, and Chardonnay in the preceding chapters, I did not mention that multiple wines in each class are offered at Wagner's. The Wagner tasting menu starts with four Rieslings of varying degrees of sweetness, two Gewürztraminers, and three Chardonnays (with and without oak influence).

The following are my recipes that can be paired with the various Wagner wines. The Wagner wine I would choose to accompany each menu item is listed below the recipe title. Most are recipes that I have developed over my years as a chef. Some are borrowed, but altered by me. I have served all of them with great success. Look for a summary of the Wine and Cheese pairings following the dessert section.

Bon appetit!

APPETIZERS & SALADS

Buffalo Meatballs
(Serve with Fathom 107)

I was in a restaurant years ago in Kingston, Ontario. Their chicken style meatballs were so good that I developed my own recipe. I've served them at my Holiday Party ever since.

Shopping Cart:
- 2 tablespoons olive oil
- 1/2 cup (1 stick) unsalted butter
- 3/4 cup Frank's Red Hot Sauce (or other hot sauce), plus more for serving
- 2 pounds ground chicken, preferably thigh meat
- 2 large eggs
- 2 ribs celery, minced (about 1 cup)
- 1 2/3 cups dried breadcrumbs (I always use Panko brand)
- 2 teaspoons coarse (kosher or sea) salt
- Blue cheese dressing
- Celery sticks for serving

Directions:

1. Preheat oven 450°F. Coat a large, rimmed baking sheet with olive oil and set aside.

2. Place butter and hot sauce in a small saucepan over low heat. Cook, whisking, until butter is melted and hot sauce is well incorporated. Remove from heat and transfer to a large bowl; let cool to room temperature, about 10 minutes

3. Add chicken, eggs, celery, breadcrumbs, and salt to bowl with melted butter mixture; using your hands, mix until well combined. Roll chicken mixture into firm, 1" round balls and place on prepared baking sheet; arrange the meatballs in rows so that they are touching on all sides. Transfer to oven and bake until cooked through, about 15 minutes.

4. Remove from oven. Let stand about 5 minutes before removing from baking sheet. Place on a serving platter and drizzle with hot sauce.

5. Serve with blue cheese dressing and celery sticks.

Caesar Salad
(Serve with Reserve Chardonnay)

The Caesar Salad was first tossed by Caesar Cardini at the Hotel Comercial in Tijuana, Mexico, around 1924. Cardini had run out of some of his salad ingredients, so he used what he had on hand, inventing this timeless salad in the process. He moved his restaurant and the salad recipe to the newly constructed Caesar Hotel in 1929. The restaurant and hotel are still in operation today. I enjoyed my first Caesar Salad there in 1978. My daughter says that I make the world's best Caesar. You can decide for yourselves!

Shopping Cart for Dressing:
(This makes a lot of dressing, but it stores well in the fridge.)
- 1 1/2 cups extra virgin olive oil
- 2 cups freshly grated Parmesan cheese
- Juice of 7 lemons
- 1 teaspoon Dijon mustard
- Dash Worcestershire Sauce
- 2 tablespoons mayonnaise

Combine the dressing ingredients, preferably in a blender.

Shopping Cart for Salad:

- One large head of romaine lettuce
- 1 tablespoons extra virgin olive oil
- Freshly ground pepper, to taste (the more, the better!)
- 1 teaspoons crushed garlic (more, to taste)
- Anchovy paste, to taste (optional)
- Cooked bacon (cook until crunchy), about 2 pieces per person
- Croutons
- Freshly grated Parmesan cheese, to taste

Directions:

1. Pour about one tablespoon of olive oil into a large bowl. (Traditionally, a wooden bowl is used.)
2. Add pepper and a teaspoon of crushed garlic, (and if you like—anchovy paste). Mash together with a fork.
3. Eliminate the core of the Romaine. Tear the lettuce into bite-sized pieces. (Tear enough lettuce to fill each bowl, using individual salad bowls as a guide,) Add to the large bowl.
4. Crumble the cooked, crisp bacon—about 2 pieces per person. Add to the large bowl.
5. Toss to combine Romaine, crumbled bacon, and oil mixture.

6. Add dressing to this mixture, to taste. (Don't add too much dressing or it will get soggy.)
7. Add and lightly toss croutons—one or two tosses will do.
8. Place salad in bowls. Sprinkle with grated Parmesan cheese.

Greek Salad
(Serve with Rosé of Cabernet Franc)

My father's parents emigrated from Greece and met in New York City. Dad loved this Greek salad.

Shopping Cart:
- 4 medium, juicy tomatoes, preferably heirloom
- 1 English (hot house) cucumber
- 1 green bell pepper, cored
- 1 medium red onion
- Pitted Greek Kalamata olives
- A pinch of salt
- 4 tablespoons extra virgin olive oil
- 1–2 tablespoons red wine vinegar
- 1/2 cup Greek feta cheese, diced
- 1/2 tablespoon dried oregano
- Crusty, crusty FRESH bread

Directions:

1. Cut the tomatoes into wedges or large chunks.
2. Cut cucumber in half length-wise, then cut into thick slices (at least 1/2" in thickness).
3. Thinly slice the bell pepper into rings.
4. Cut the red onion in half and thinly slice into half moons.
5. Place everything in a large salad bowl. Add a good handful of the pitted Kalamata olives.
6. Sprinkle with a pinch of salt. Top with the olive oil and red wine vinegar.
7. Give everything a very gentle toss to mix. Do NOT over mix! This salad is not meant to be handled too much.
8. Top with the feta chunks. Sprinkle with the dried oregano.
9. Serve with crusty bread.

Beef & Poultry
Beef Short Ribs Provençale
(Serve with Cabernet Franc)

Every once in awhile, even the best chefs—and I am far from a "best chef"—find a recipe that they can't find major fault with. I've made very few, minor changes to this recipe, which was developed by Rick Rogers (The Carefree Cook). It appeared in a 2003 issue of Bon Appétit Magazine.

Shopping Cart:
- 2 tablespoons extra virgin olive oil
- 6 pounds individual beef short ribs
- 3/4 teaspoon Kosher salt
- 1/2 teaspoon freshly ground black pepper
- 1 large onion, finely chopped
- 1 medium carrot, finely chopped
- 1 celery rib, finely chopped
- 12 garlic cloves, peeled
- 1 tablespoon Herbes de Provence
- 2 tablespoon all-purpose flour
- 2 cups Wagner Cabernet Franc

(continued)

- 1 3/4 cups beef stock
- One 14 ½ oz. can diced tomatoes, drained
- 1 bay leaf
- 8 oz. baby-cut carrots
- 1/2 cup Mediterranean black olives (pitted)
- Fresh parsley for garnish
- Fresh, crusty bread

Directions:

1. Preheat oven to 300°F.

2. Heat oil in a large (ovenproof) Dutch oven over medium-high heat. Season short ribs with the salt and pepper. In batches, add the short ribs to the pot and cook, turning, until brown on all sides (about 10 minutes). Remove ribs to a platter.

3. Pour off all but 2 tbsp of the fat from the pot. Add the onion, chopped carrot, and celery to the pot and reduce the heat to medium-low. Cover, stir often, and cook until vegetables are softened.

4. Add the garlic, Herbs de Province, and flour; stir until you can smell the garlic (about a minute). Stir in the wine and bring to a boil over high

heat. Stir up the bits stuck to the bottom of the pot.

5. Add the broth, tomatoes, and bay leaf.
6. Return the ribs and any juices to the pot. Add cold water if necessary to almost cover the top of the ribs. Bring to a boil over high heat.
7. Cover tightly, transfer to the oven and bake, stirring occasionally, until the meat is falling off the bones (about 2½ hours). During the last 15 minutes, add the baby carrots.
8. Transfer the ribs to a deep serving platter and cover with foil to keep warm.
9. Skim off the fat, and discard the bay leaf. Bring to a boil, over high heat, and reduce to a sauce consistency—about 10 minutes. Add the olives and heat for 3 additional minutes. Season with salt and pepper. Spoon the sauce over the ribs.
10. Sprinkle with parsley and serve with fresh, crusty bread.

Beef Tenderloin with Mushroom Sauce
(Serve with Pinot Noir Grace House)

The King of Reds demands the King of Beef. When I was young, our family frequented Pierce's 1894 Restaurant in Elmira Heights, NY, just a 20-minute drive from our home. In its heyday, it was considered one of the finest restaurants in America. The most elegant item on their menu was their Chateaubriand, a baked beef tenderloin. At Pierce's, this masterpiece was wheeled to your table on a cart. The owner came out to slice it, topping it with a classic Béarnaise sauce. It was all very impressive.

Filet mignon is grilled beef tenderloin. It is the most tender cut of beef. Perhaps nothing summons a great Pinot Noir pairing quite like a roasted beef tenderloin or filet mignon.

Shopping Cart:
- 1 (2 to 3 pound) beef tenderloin
- Virgin olive oil
- 2 teaspoons sugar
- Kosher salt, to taste
- ½ cup black peppercorns (crushed with mortar & pestle)

Directions:

1. Preheat oven to 475°
2. Make sure the tenderloin is trimmed of fat. The tenderloin tapers to a very small section. Take that section and fold it under the upper tenderloin and tie it with string, making the entire tenderloin look uniform. Rub the tenderloin with oil, then with the salt and sugar.
3. Pressed the crushed pepper into the entire surface of the tenderloin.
4. Place on a rack in a baking pan.
5. Roast for about 20 minutes. (It does not take nearly as long as you might think.) Meat thermometer should read 125°. Remove from oven.
6. THIS IS IMPORTANT. Let it sit for at least 10 minutes before slicing, to let the juices seal.
7. Slice to preferred thickness.
8. Top with Mushroom Sauce (recipe follows).

Mushroom Sauce

As mentioned, I believe that mushrooms were "invented" to go with Pinot Noir.

Shopping Cart:

- 2 tablespoons unsalted butter
- 1/2 tablespoons olive oil
- 10 oz. assorted mushrooms, sliced
- Pinch of salt and pepper
- 2 garlic cloves, minced
- 1/4 cup Wagner Pinot Noir
- 1/2 cup (125 ml) beef broth
- 1 cup (250 ml) heavy cream
- 1/2 cup grated parmesan cheese
- 2 teaspoons fresh thyme leaves, chopped (or 1/4 - 1/2 teaspoons dried)

Directions:

1. Heat oil and melt butter in a skillet over medium high heat. Add mushrooms and cook until golden brown.
2. Add the garlic and salt & pepper just as the mushrooms are finished, stir until the fragrance of the garlic is evident.

3. Add the Pinot Noir. Stir, scraping particles, until slightly evaporated.
4. Lower heat to medium, add broth, cream and cheese. Stir, do not let boil. Continue to stir for a few minutes, until it thickens.
5. Add thyme, and adjust salt and pepper.
6. Top sliced tenderloin with sauce

Wine Country Burger
with Béarnaise Mayonnaise & Red Onion Marmalade
(Serve with Cabernet Sauvignon)

From 1985 to 2007, I managed and operated our family restaurant, Chef's Diner, between Montour Falls and Watkins Glen. In 1992, I instituted my "Burger of the Week," each week developing a new burger with various herbs, spices, toppings and sauces. In the next 15 years I developed over 200 different burgers. I always thought about writing a book about burgers, perhaps I will now. The following is one of my favorites, one of the most involved, and one of the most popular. Note: This is a four-napkin burger!

Shopping Cart for the Burger:
- 1 1/2 lb. good ground beef or sirloin, shaped into 4 six-ounce patties.
- 4 thick slices of New York white cheddar cheese
- 4 large, bakery-fresh hard rolls

Directions:

1. Grill burger to medium-rare (longer for sissies who don't like bloody burgers!)
2. Top with cheddar cheese during last 3 min. of grilling
3. Place burgers on hard rolls.
4. Top burgers with red onion marmalade and the béarnaise mayonnaise.

Béarnaise Mayonnaise

Shopping Cart:

- 1/3 cup Wagner's Caywood East Riesling
- 1 tablespoon white wine vinegar
- 2 minced shallots
- 1 cup mayonnaise
- 1 tablespoon chopped fresh tarragon
- 1 teaspoon grated lemon rind
- 1/8 teaspoon pepper

Directions:

1. In a small saucepan, combine the Riesling, white wine vinegar and minced shallots. Cook over medium heat for 5 minutes or until

liquid is reduced to about 1 tbsp. Remove from heat. Cool.

2. Stir together mayonnaise, chopped fresh tarragon, grated lemon rind, pepper, and the wine reduction liquid.

Red Onion Marmalade

Shopping Cart:

- 4 red onions, sliced
- 1 tablespoon butter
- ½ cup dark brown sugar
- ½ cup Wagner's Cabernet Sauvignon

Directions:

1. Put sliced onions in a pot with a cover. Add the butter. Cover. Cook over low heat until the onions are soft and steaming. (This can take 30 min. to an hour.)
2. Remove cover, stir in brown sugar, turn heat to high. Stir often.
3. After 15 min. add the Cabernet Sauvignon.
4. Cook briefly to let the wine permeate the caramelized onions.

Chicken Française
(Serve with Dry Riesling)

There are many variations of this dish. It became very popular in Rochester, New York where Italian immigrants would substitute chicken for veal (Veal Française) and eventually call it Chicken French. Some even called it Chicken Rochester. This is just perfect with the Wagner Vineyards Dry Riesling.

Shopping Cart:
- 4 to 6 boneless, skinless chicken breast (sliced or pounded-out, into 1/4-in thick pieces)
- 4 eggs, plus 2 tablespoon milk (beaten)
- 1 cup flour
- 1 tablespoon salt
- 1 teaspoon black pepper
- Cayenne to taste
- 2 tablespoons olive oil plus 1 tablespoon butter (for sautéing)

For the Sauce:
- Juice of two lemons
- 1/2 cup Wagner Dry Riesling
- 1 cup chicken stock
- 4 tablespoons cold butter (cut into cubes)
- 1 tablespoon chopped Italian parsley
- Salt and fresh ground black pepper (to taste)

Directions:

1. Season chicken pieces on both sides with salt and fresh ground black pepper. Place the flour, salt, pepper, and cayenne in a baking dish and mix well.

2. Combine the beaten eggs and milk in another dish. Dredge the chicken, one at a time, in the flour to coat both sides and then transfer into the dish of eggs. Turn the chicken in the egg to coat both sides, and leave in the egg.

3. Once all the chicken is floured and transferred into the dish of eggs, place in the refrigerator until needed. In a large non-stick skillet, melt the butter in the olive oil over med-low heat, until it begins to sizzle slightly.

Lift the chicken pieces out of the egg mixture, allowing the excess to drip off, and sauté for 2 to 3 minutes per side until golden brown. Cook in batches and keep warm in a very low oven.

4. When all the chicken is cooked, add the lemon juice, wine, and broth to the pan. Bring to a boil over high heat until reduced by half. Turn off the pan, and add the parsley and cold butter to the pan. Whisk until the butter melts. Taste for salt and pepper, and adjust.

5. Place the chicken on warm plates and spoon over the sauce. Serve immediately.

PORK/LAMB
Choucroute Garnie
(Alsatian Pork and Sauerkraut Stew)
(Serve with Dry Gewürztraminer)

Several years ago, I did a vertical wine tasting during January and February. I paired current vintages of wine with wines from our "library" of wines that we save for special occasions. The wines were paired with cheese, chocolate, and a hot dish. When I used Gewürztraminer from four different vintages, the hot dish was Choucroute Garnie, a sausage-style stew that dates to 15th Century Alsace. The word "choucroute" is French for "sauerkraut," but since the 20th Century it usually refers to the Alsatian dish, choucroute garnie, with its concoction of sauerkraut braised in white wine and an assortment of sausages, ham, fresh and smoked pork, steamed potatoes, and a dash of mustard. The dish is washed down with the local wine, and for this, I used Gewürztraminer.

Shopping Cart:

- 1/4 cup duck fat (or peanut oil)
- 1 pound kielbasa
- 1 pound double-smoked slab bacon, halved lengthwise
- 12 ounces (4 links) bratwurst
- 1/2 rack (1 pound) baby back ribs, halved crosswise
- 1 pound (2 1/2 cups) sauerkraut, drained
- 1 teaspoon juniper berries (or rosemary)
- 1 teaspoon whole black peppercorns
- 10 whole cloves
- 4 cloves garlic, thinly sliced
- 3 bay leaves
- 1$^{1/2}$ cups chicken stock
- 1½ cups dry white wine (Gewurztraminer)
- 1 pound baby red-skin potatoes
- Assorted mustards, for serving
- Crusty bread, for serving

(continued)

Directions:

1. In an 8-quart Dutch oven, heat the duck fat or peanut oil over medium-high heat. Working in batches, cook the kielbasa, bacon, bratwurst and ribs, turning as needed, until golden brown, 4 to 6 minutes for the kielbasa and bacon, and 6 to 8 minutes for the bratwurst and ribs. Transfer each to a plate.

2. To the pot, add the sauerkraut, juniper berries, peppercorns, cloves, garlic and bay leaves. Cook until warmed through and fragrant, 3 minutes. Add the reserved meats, the stock and white wine, and bring to a simmer. Cook, covered, until the meat is tender, 1 hour. Add the potatoes and continue to cook until tender, 25 to 30 minutes more.

3. Transfer the meats to a cutting board and slice. Arrange on a platter with the braised sauerkraut and potatoes on the side, then serve with assorted mustards and crusty bread.

Roasted Leg of Lamb
(Serve with Merlot)

My mother loved lamb. We would have this throughout the year, but always on Christmas Eve.

Shopping Cart:

- 1 5 to 6 pound leg of lamb, with bone, nicely trimmed
- 1 1/2 tablespoons minced garlic
- 1 tablespoon virgin olive oil
- 1 tablespoons chopped fresh rosemary
- 1 tablespoon chopped fresh thyme leaves
- 1 tablespoon Dijon mustard
- 1 tablespoon sea salt
- 2 teaspoon ground black pepper

Directions:

1. Preheat oven to 350°F
2. Line a roasting pan with aluminum foil.
3. Pat lamb dry with paper towels. With a sharp knife, score the top side of the lamb by making shallow cuts all over.

(continued)

4. In a small bowl, combine garlic, olive oil, rosemary, thyme, Dijon mustard, salt and pepper.

5. Place lamb, fat side up, on a rack in the prepared roasting pan. Spread garlic mixture evenly over the lamb, rubbing garlic mixture thoroughly into the scored lamb.

6. Place pan in oven. Roast until internal temperature reaches 135°F for medium (about $1^{1/2}$ to $1^{3/4}$ hours), or longer if desired.

7. Let the lamb rest 15 min. before slicing.

SEAFOOD

Crab Cakes
with Lemon Aioli Sauce
(Serve with Caywood East)

Historians tell us that the practice of making minced meat cakes is ancient. Minces mixed with bread, spices, and fillers came about for two reasons: taste and economy. Primary evidence suggests recipes for crab-cake types dishes were introduced in the New World by English settlers. A survey of historic American cookbooks confirms that crab recipes have been popular since colonial days.

In the 19th Century, crab recipes proliferated. Many of these included a combination of bread crumbs and spices; some were fried. Sometimes they stand alone, others are noted as possible variations under similar fish or shellfish recipes. The phrase "crab cake" appears to be a 20th Century appellation. "Crab cake: a sautéed or fried patty of crabmeat." The term dates in print to 1930 in

Crosby Gaige's New York World's Fair Cook Book, where they are called "Baltimore crab cakes," suggesting they have long been known in the South. This, my recipe, was the most popular appetizer that I served in my catering business.

Shopping Cart:

- 1 lb. fresh lump crabmeat
- $2^{1/2}$ cups Panko bread crumbs
- 1 egg beaten
- 3/4 cup mayonnaise
- 1/3 cup finely chopped celery
- 1/3 cup finely diced green bell pepper
- 1/3 cup finely chopped green onions
- 1/2 tablespoon Old Bay seasoning
- 1/2 tablespoon Creole seasoning
- 1 tablespoon minced fresh parsley
- 1 tablespoon lemon juice
- 2 teaspoons Dijon mustard
- 1/4 teaspoon black pepper
- Dash of hot pepper sauce

For Lemon Aioli Sauce:
- 1 egg yolk
- 2 teaspoons Dijon
- 1 teaspoon white wine vinegar
- 1 teaspoon fresh lemon juice
- 1/4 teaspoon kosher salt
- pinch cayenne
- 1/4 cup olive oil

Directions:

1. Combine all ingredients in a bowl, adding crab meat and Panko bread crumbs last. Mix by hand or with a spatula.
2. Using a 1/3 cup measure, place (pack) crab mixture into the measuring cup and invert on a wax paper lined baking sheet. (You will have to tap the 1/3 cup on the sheet to drop the crab mixture out.) If the mixture falls apart, put it back in the bowl and add a little more mayo to hold it together. If the mixture holds its shape, you are all set. Repeat with the remaining mixture.

3. Cover with plastic wrap and freeze the ones that you are not using. (When frozen, you can bag them.)

4. To cook: Put a very small amount of oil in the bottom of a non-stick skillet. Heat oil to medium high. Sauté about two minutes per side. They will be golden brown. Top with Aioli sauce.

Directions for Lemon Aioli Sauce

Put first six items in a blender and blend, slowly add the oil while the blender is on until it is the consistency of mayonnaise.

Live Lobster
Boiled or Steamed
(Serve with Sparkling Riesling)

If you do not have a 4 to 5 gallon pot, stop here. Buy one or forget cooking a live lobster!

The big question is: Should live lobsters be boiled or steamed?

Most grocery store lobster tanks are filled with lobsters that range in size from a pound and a quarter to 3 pounds (or more). If lobsters are "in season," many supermarkets offer specials for their smaller lobsters, sometimes $6.99 a pound. They average between $12.99 and $14.99 a pound during the remainder of the year. Two-pound lobsters are perfect. Contrary to rumors you may have heard, the meat of larger lobsters is every bit as delicious as that of smaller ones. However, it can be challenging to remove the meat from the thicker shells of large lobsters. (I have actually taken the claws outside, wrapped them in a towel, and used a hammer to crack them open!)

I prefer a female lobster to a male. The tails on females tend to be larger, and the claws smaller. The tails of female lobsters contain roe (the tasty eggs). You can ask for female lobsters; if the person at the seafood counter is knowledgeable, they will know by looking.

Shopping Cart:

- 2 Live lobsters (2 pounders, if possible)
- Melted butter (lots of it)
- Lemon wedges

"Experts" (I love that word) are divided over the best way to cook a live lobster. Almost every website that sells Maine lobsters, delivered alive to your home, recommends boiling. But you can find ten opinions from other sites, and there is no definitive answer.

I prefer boiling. Boiling a lobster is the easiest way to cook and serve a whole lobster. A boiled lobster is also easier to pick clean. If you are cooking a lot of lobsters for a summer outing, boiling is always the best method.

Steaming is a more gentle process of cooking the meat and many chefs insist that steaming preserves more flavor and tenderness. Steaming a lobster is also more forgiving on the chef since it is harder to overcook a lobster in a steam pot.

Directions for Boiling:

1. Fill large pot with water. Add 1/4 cup sea salt for each gallon of water. (Remember that the lobsters will displace some water, so do not fill to the very top.)
2. Cover the pot. Bring to a rolling boil.
3. Place LIVE lobsters in, head-first, cover.
4. Let water return to a boil, then reduce heat to medium.

(continued)

5. After water returns to a boil, I usually cook for 12 minutes for the smaller lobsters (1$^{1/2}$ lbs.), 15 minutes for the two pounders, and 25 minutes for three pounders.
6. Carefully, remove lobsters with tongs. Allow the lobsters to sit for 5 to 10 minutes to cool.
7. Serve with butter and lemon wedges.

Directions for Steaming:

1. Add 2 inches of water to a pot. Cover
2. Bring water to a rolling boil.
3. Place the Maine lobsters in the pot, cover tightly.
4. When the water returns to a heavy boil, turn the heat down, but maintain a rolling boil.
5. Steam lobsters for 9 minutes for the first pound, adding 4 minutes for each additional pound.
6. Steamed lobsters will be bright red when done.
7. Remove the steamed lobsters with tongs, let cool for 3-5 minutes.
8. Serve with melted butter and lemon wedges.

Setting the Table for Your Lobster Dinner

I try to have lobster at least once a month. I always save a Sunday newspaper, which I spread over the table like a tablecloth. (I learned this trick at an all-you-could-eat soft-shelled crab place in Florida about 50 years ago). Make sure your plates are large enough to hold a whole lobster. I put a ramekin or small bowl next to each plate to hold the melted butter. In addition to a fork and sharp knife, each setting includes a lobster or nut cracker, a small "pick" to remove the lobster meat from the smaller parts of the lobster and, if desired, a pair of kitchen shears. The table will also have a roll of paper towels and a large bowl to put the shells in. A hurricane candle holder and some flowers add a nice touch.

Mussels
(Serve with Unoaked Chardonnay)

Think that you don't like mussels? Try this recipe. Mussels are very inexpensive and relatively easy to prepare. DON'T FORGET THE LOAF OF CRUSTY BREAD TO DIP IN THE SAUCE!

Shopping Cart:

- 4 pounds live mussels
- 2 cups Unoaked Wagner Chardonnay
- 4 large shallots, finely chopped
- 4 cloves garlic, finely chopped
- 1/2 teaspoon salt
- 1/3 cup mixed fresh herbs (such as flat-leaf parsley, chervil, or basil, chopped)
- 6 tablespoons butter, cut into pieces
- A nice loaf of crusty, baguette-style bread

Directions:

1. Rinse and scrub mussels under cold water.
2. Using your fingers or paring knife, remove beards (strings that hang from the mussel shells),
3. Combine wine, shallots, garlic and salt in a large stockpot (with a lid). Bring to boil. Simmer 5 minutes.
4. Add mussels, cover and increase heat to high.
5. Cook until all mussels are open, about 5 minutes.
6. Stir in herbs and butter.
7. Remove from heat.
8. Divide mussels and broth among four bowls.

Serve immediately with lots of bread to sop up the sauce!

Pan Seared Salmon
(Serve with Barrel Fermented Chardonnay)

There are countless ways to prepare salmon, which is a relatively inexpensive seafood, and so good for you.

Shopping Cart:
- 4 6-ounce skin-on salmon filets
- 1 1/2 medium lemons
- 4 cloves garlic, minced
- 2 tablespoons chopped fresh parsley leaves
- 1 teaspoon kosher salt
- 2 tablespoons olive oil
- 8 tablespoons (1 stick) unsalted butter

Directions:
1. Juice one of the lemons until you have 2 tablespoons juice. Cut the remaining 1/2 lemon into 4 wedges for serving.
2. Put the salmon on a plate or cutting board, skin side down. Pat dry with a paper towel.
3. Sprinkle the kosher salt over the salmon.

4. In large frying pan, heat olive oil on medium high. Add the salmon skin-side up and sear until golden-brown on the bottom, about 4 minutes.
5. Flip the salmon. Add the butter and garlic. Continue to cook, occasionally spooning the liquid over the salmon. Cook until the salmon is just cooked, about 4 minutes more.
6. Sprinkle with the parsley and drizzle with the lemon juice. Serve with the lemon wedges.

Sautéed Scallops with Riesling Reduction
(Serve with Semi-Dry Riesling)

This is a high-end menu item at those fancy restaurants you frequent when you have a special birthday or just want to treat yourself. Until you try to prepare scallops, you have no idea how easy it is and how good they are, and how everyone will think that you are a brilliant chef.

Shopping Cart:
- 1/3 cup Wagner semi-dry Riesling
- 3 tablespoons water
- 2 tablespoons minced fresh onion
- 1 garlic clove, minced
- 1 teaspoon Dijon mustard
- ½ teaspoon oregano
- 1 pound sea scallops
- ½ teaspoon salt
- ½ teaspoon freshly ground black pepper
- 2 teaspoons virgin olive oil
- 2 tablespoons butter
- 2 tablespoons chopped fresh parsley

Directions:

1. Combine the first six ingredients.
2. Wash scallops well and remove that small membrane that holds the scallop to the shell.
3. Sprinkle scallops with salt and pepper.
4. Heat oil in a large skillet until hot, medium-high heat. Cook scallops about two minutes per side – until each side is slightly browned.
5. Remove scallops and tent with foil – they will continue to cook – so be careful not to overcook in the pan.
6. Pour wine mixture into pan, cook over medium-high heat. Bring to a boil, and cook until reduced (to about 1/3 cup). Remove from heat and stir in butter.
7. Plate scallops and spoon sauce over—top with parsley. Serve—and prepare to be called a culinary genius!

Pasta

Smoked Gouda Carbonara
(Serve with Semi-Dry Gewürztraminer)

Shopping Cart:
- 1 lb. spaghetti
- 5 large egg yolks
- 1 large egg
- 1 cup (4 oz.) finely shredded smoked Gouda
- Kosher salt and black pepper, to taste
- 1 tablespoon extra-virgin olive oil
- 6 oz. slab bacon, finely diced
- 3/4 teaspoon crushed red pepper
- Additional shredded Gouda to sprinkle on finished pasta.

Directions:
1. Bring a large pot of salted water to a rolling boil. Add the spaghetti to the water, slowly so that the water continues to boil. Cook until al dente or to desired doneness.

2. Drain, reserving 2 cups of the cooking water. (You may not need all of the water.)
3. In a large bowl, beat the egg yolks with the whole egg.
4. Stir in the shredded Gouda, salt and black pepper.
5. Very gradually whisk in 1/2 cup of the reserved cooking water. (This "tempers" the eggs.)
6. Heat the olive oil in the pot in which you cooked the pasta. Add the bacon and cook over moderate heat until rendered but not crisp, 5 to 7 minutes.
7. Return the pasta to the pot. Add the crushed red pepper and 1/4 cup of the reserved pasta cooking water.
8. Cook, tossing, until the pasta is coated, 1 to 2 minutes. Scrape the pasta mixture into the large bowl and toss vigorously until creamy, 1 to 2 minutes, adding more cooking water if needed. Season with salt and pepper.
9. Divide the pasta into bowls and serve, passing additional shredded cheese at the table.

DESSERT

Apple Pie
(Serve with Riesling Select)

Apple pies are very time consuming. This one will be worth your time and trouble.

Shopping Cart:
- 3/4 cup sugar
- 3 tablespoons cornstarch
- 1 teaspoon ground cinnamon
- ½ teaspoon salt
- 1 package pre-made Pillsbury pie crust (contains 2 sheets for bottom and top crusts (or make your own)
- All-purpose flour for rolling
- 8 medium apples (about 3 ½ pounds) peeled, cored, and cut into one-quarter inch slices. A mixture of different apples is good (Honeycrisp, Fuji, and Granny Smith, for example).

Directions:

1. Preheat oven to 400°F.
2. In a large bowl whisk together the sugar, cornstarch, cinnamon and salt.
3. On a lightly floured surface unroll one of the dough crusts into a 13" round and place inside a 9" pie plate. Unroll the other disk.
4. Add the apples to the sugar mixture and toss thoroughly. (Do this at the LAST minute, not before rolling disk.) Pour mixture into the pie shell. Cover with the other shell and crimp the edges. Cut about a dozen slits all over the top crust of the pie.
5. Sprinkle liberally with cinnamon and sugar, and place on a baking sheet lined with aluminum foil.
6. Bake until the crust is golden brown and the filling is bubbly (65 to 75 minutes). Cool on a rack.

Chocolate Covered Strawberries
(Serve with Meritage)

This is something that everyone loves on Valentine's Day. Now you can make your own, anytime. Decadent? Yes! The perfect complement to Meritage!

Shopping Cart:
- Fresh, plump, red strawberries
- Bittersweet or semi-sweet chocolate chips, 12 ounces or more. (The better the chocolate, the better your strawberries will be.)
- For toppings, your choice: melted white chocolate, chopped nuts (peanuts, pistachios, pecans, etc.), toasted coconut, sprinkles, graham cracker crumbs, crushed Oreo cookies, crushed candy canes

Directions:
1. Wash and WELL-dry the strawberries.
2. Prepare desired toppings (nuts, toasted coconut, etc.)

3. Prepare your workspace with a parchment lined baking tray to place the dipped strawberries on.

4. Melt the chocolate in a double boiler (my preference) or a microwave. Stir until very smooth. A double boiler allows you to keep the chocolate warm.

5. Dip the strawberries in melted chocolate.

6. Coat in desired toppings.

7. Lay the strawberries on prepared baking sheet and allow them to rest until the chocolate has set.

8. If desired, drizzle with melted white chocolate.

Pots de Crème au Chocolat
(Serve with Vidal & Riesling Dessert Wines)

Great story here. (Great dessert here, too.)

I met my editor, Donna Himelfarb, in 2016. A few months after we met, she took me to Gilda's, a popular eatery in Skaneateles, NY. She had hoped to introduce me to her favorite dessert, Pots de Crème au Chocolat. The manager, Donna's friend, Peter Bettis, told us that the new chef was having problems perfecting the Pots de Crème, so it was no longer on the menu. (It eventually returned, perfectly prepared.)

I went home and researched many recipes and created one for Donna. Baking it in a water bath is tricky and you have to watch it carefully. I proudly presented the Pots de Crème to Donna, who may be the most straightforward person that I have ever known. She told me that there was something wrong with the custard. It was "gritty." When you look at the directions, you will see that I have highlighted how important it is to run the melted chocolate through a fine mesh screen. I hadn't thought it was necessary, so I had skipped that step. Never again!

Shopping Cart:
- 2 cups whipping cream
- 1/2 cup whole milk
- 5 ounces bittersweet (not unsweetened) or semisweet chocolate, finely chopped
- 6 large egg yolks
- 1/3 cup sugar
- Extra cream, whipped, for topping

Directions:
1. Preheat oven to 325°F. Bring cream and milk just to simmer in heavy medium saucepan over medium heat. Remove from heat.
2. Add chocolate; whisk until melted and smooth.

(continued)

3. Whisk yolks and sugar in large bowl to blend.

4. Gradually whisk in hot chocolate mixture. (If you add it too fast, the eggs will cook and ruin the recipe.

5. Strain mixture into another bowl. (THIS IS IMPORTANT, use a fine mesh screen). Cool 10 minutes, skim any foam from surface.

6. Divide custard mixture among six 3/4-cup ramekins or soufflé dishes. Cover each with foil.

7. Place cups in large baking pan. Add enough hot water to the pan to come halfway up sides of cups. Bake until custards are set, but centers still move slightly when gently shaken, about 55 minutes.

8. Remove from water. Remove foil. Chill custards until cold, about 3 hours.

9. Top with freshly whipped cream.

Wine and Cheese:
Matches Made in Heaven!

Riesling:
Ricotta, Jarlsberg, Camembert, Gruyere

Gewürztraminer:
Muenster, soft cow milk cheese

Chardonnay:
Fontina, Camembert, goat cheese, blue cheese

Cabernet Franc:
Goat Cheese, Camembert, Feta, Fontina

Cabernet Sauvignon:
Aged cheddar or Gouda

Merlot:
Gorgonzola, Brie, Jarlsberg, or Parmesan.

Pinot Noir:
Gouda, Gruyere, Taleggio, Cheddar

Sparkling Riesling:
Triple Cream and Marscapone

Rosé:
Goat Cheese

Ice Wine:
Aged Cheddar, Brie, Mascarpone

Meritgage:
Mild and medium sharp Cheddar, Edam, Muenster,
Smoked Gouda

Fathom 107:
Muenster, soft cow milk cheese

APPENDICES

Appendix I: Phylloxera

Phylloxera is a tiny aphid-like bug (about 1/30th of an inch long) that almost caused the extinction of the prized Vitus Vinifera grape (the grapes of the Mediterranean, Central Europe, southwestern Asia, from Morocco to Portugal, northward to southern Germany, and east to northern Iran).

This native American insect destroys grapevines by attacking their roots. The American Vitis Labrusca vines and roots (Catawba, Concord, Delaware, Isabella, Niagara, and others) are naturally resistant to the pest. The real damage didn't begin until the bugs latched onto the roots of the European Vitis Vinifera vines.

By the mid 1800s, Europeans had developed a fondness for our corn and turkey, leading them to request the "foxy" taste of our native American grapes. These grapes were first imported to Europe in the 1860s, but modern procedures for importing and exporting of agricultural products had not been established yet. The Phylloxera insect was a stowaway on the roots of the American grapes that were sent to Europe. Once they were introduced to foreign soil, they quickly and mercilessly attacked the European grapevines' roots, destroying the vines of Vinifera grapes.

The mouth of the Phylloxera aphid has both a venom canal, from which it injects its deadly venom, and a feeding tube, through which it takes in vine sap and nutrients. As the toxin from the venom corrodes the root structure of a vine, the sap pressure within the vine falls. As its sap supply weakens, the Phylloxera simply withdraws its feeding tube and searches for another host. Anyone digging up a diseased and dying vine will not find Phylloxera clinging to the roots of the plant because the insect will have already moved on to its next victim.

This unique American bug nearly destroyed the European wine industry and all the Vinifera grapes that we covet today. France is thought to have lost six million acres of vineyards. Germany, Italy, Spain and nearly every other European country were not spared.

Phylloxera also spread to Australia, New Zealand and South Africa. When he left the White House, Thomas Jefferson transplanted his beloved Chardonnay grapes to Monticello, his Virginia plantation. All of the vines died. Jefferson believed that his plantation workers had planted them incorrectly or that he had been sent diseased grapes. It was, of course, Phylloxera. California winemakers, who imported European Viniferas in the 1870s, suffered the same fate.

In the May 1874 journal, Popular Science, Charles V. Riley, Ph.D., wrote:

The genus Phylloxera is characterized by having three-jointed antennae, the third or terminal much the longest, and by carrying its wings overlapping flat on the back instead of roof-fashion. It belongs to the whole-winged bugs (Homoptera), and osculates between two great families of that sub-order, the plant-lice (Aphididae) on the one hand and the bark-lice (Coccidae) on the other. In the one-jointed tarsus of the larva or newly-hatched louse, and in being always oviparous, it shows its affinities with the latter family; but in the two-jointed tarsus of the more mature individuals, and in all other characters, it is essentially aphididan.

When Phylloxera was finally identified by Riley and others in the late 1800s, and method upon method failed to destroy the pest, vineyard masters burned their families' ancient vineyards in hopes of killing "the disease." The French Minister of Agriculture offered the equivalent of $1 million in today's dollars to anyone who found a cure.

In addition to burning the vineyards, some tried flooding, importing different soils, using poison, and trying various test plantings. Hundreds of articles and solutions were published between 1868 and

1871. Then, a Frenchman, Jules Émile Planchon, along with Riley, discovered a solution—but not a cure. They considered grafting the European grapevines to American root stock. French viticulturists imported assorted American root stock onto which they could graft their Vinifera vines. Some American rootstock did not thrive in the chalky French soils and became unable to fight off the Phylloxera from which they had previously been resistant.

After much trial and error, a sufficient number of American vines were found that could grow in the French soil. The process worked and the European wine industry was saved.

Thomas Volney Munson, a viticulturist from Texas, had provided native Texan rootstocks which were grafted successfully. In 1888, because of Munson's role in rescuing France's wine industry, the French government sent a delegation to Denison, Texas, to confer upon him the French Legion of Honor, Chevalier du Mérite Agricole. (Thomas Edison is the only other American to receive this honor.) But what about that million-dollar reward? Although Planchon and Riley did not apply for it, another French viticulturist did. Leo Laliman, who sold the newly created vines that utilized American root stock *did* apply for the prize. Sadly for him, the French government declined to give him the reward because he played no role in solving the problem.

With the solution to the Phylloxera nightmare, vintners, vineyard managers, and owners rejoiced. Although no cure had been discovered, the immediate problem had been solved. The American rootstock, grafted to their beloved Vinifera grapes, was a success.

Problem solved? Not so fast. The rejoicing ended nearly a century later, when, in 1983, a new strain of Phylloxera emerged in California, eventually spreading to Oregon and Washington. The root stock used in those areas had been resistant for years, but it was discovered that the root stock had parent vines containing the DNA of Vinifera grapes. Entire vineyards were ripped up and replanted.

It takes three to five years for newly planted grapes to be mature enough for wine-making. This latest incident showed the wine industry that, until an actual cure is found, no one is ever truly safe from Phylloxera. As a result, most of the world's grapes today are grafted to American root stock.

Regardless of whether you purchase a bottle of the French Burgundy, Domaine Leroy Musigny Grand Cru for $14,436.00 or the Wagner Alta B Red for $9.99, you can be assured that the vines had American root stock. Now you know why!

Appendix II: Terroir, Microclimate and the Banana Belt

I'll try to be as clear as possible, but please remember that I am not a scientist. You cannot discuss the success of the Finger Lakes in producing world class wines without examining the terroir and the microclimate of the region.

As you have read, I steer clear of fancy "wine words" that the general public may not be able to understand. These include "full-bodied," "minerality" and more. Let me add "terroir" to that list. Now let me attempt to explain it.

Terroir is a French word that simply means earth or soil. Standing in a room full of many bottles of varied Vinifera wines and wine connoisseurs, the term terroir will always be used, especially when comparing "New World" to "Old World" wines. You know that southern California is not the southern Finger Lakes. You know that the Texas wine region is nothing like the Finger Lakes. You know that vacationing on the Atlantic Ocean in Florida in January is nothing like vacationing on Seneca Lake in the Finger Lakes in January! The difference in all of these examples is in the climate and the weather (climate and weather are *not* the same), the geography, and the soil.

It is these factors—climate, weather, geography and soil—that differentiate one region from another. These factors are the "terroir" of that region.

The climate of a region takes into account the temperature, humidity, wind, and rainfall over an extended period of time. The Finger Lakes and many other regions experience four distinct seasons. The wine regions of southern California, Spain and others do not. Thus, the terroir of the Finger Lakes does not mirror that of southern California or Spain or many of the world's other wine regions. The climate of a region dictates what types of grapes can be grown in that region. Tempranillo, the most popular grape in Spain, and the fourth most widely grown red grape in the world, cannot be grown in the Finger Lakes. The climate is not warm enough or warm *long* enough to support the grape. But Tempranillo thrives in the up-and-coming Texas wine region. Tempranillo is to Texas what Riesling is to the Finger Lakes.

Speaking of Riesling, the warm, Mediterranean-like climate of southern California does not provide the proper conditions for producing Riesling. The nights are too warm to develop the acid that Riesling needs. Thus, the "terroir" of the Napa Region does not provide the ideal growing conditions for the number one grape of the Finger Lakes. On the other hand, the terroir of the Mosel in Germany, the DNA home of the Riesling grape, is very similar to the Finger Lakes, thus the success of the Riesling grape there.

"Climate" is the long-term average of weather conditions in a particular region; "weather," on the other hand, is comprised of the day-to-day fluctuations in a region's climate. A one-day summer hail storm could destroy a crop. A hail storm is weather, not climate. We expect the summer to be warm, even hot in the Finger Lakes. It is unusual to go without rain for 12 weeks; it is also unusual for it to rain nearly every day over that period of time.

Nonetheless, the summer of 2016 saw no rain for 12 weeks. The following summer, 2017, saw a great deal of rain, but overall, perhaps the best October weather in decades. Throughout the summer of 2018 and 2019, it rained and rained and rained.

The summer of 2020 won't be recalled fondly by most of us, but it will be remembered for great wine. Indeed, if the growing season was as perfect as we believe, the wines will be extraordinary. I have often said that if you can consistently make good wine in the Finger Lakes, you can make good wine anywhere in the world!

So, terroir is the set of factors (climate, weather, soil, geography) that creates the character of wine as well as the features that distinguish a Riesling, a Chardonnay or a Cabernet from the Burgundy or Bordeaux regions vs. Napa vs. the Finger Lakes, etc.

Climate is a major component of any terroir. A *macroclimate* is the climate of a major geographic region, like the northeast of the United States, or southwest of the United States, or the climate of England or Saudi Arabia. The *microclimate* is the climate within a macroclimate. It is the climate of a very small or restricted area that differs from the climate of the surrounding area. Even within the Finger Lakes the microclimate differs. For example, on the east side of Seneca Lake, about 20 miles north of the southern end of the lake, there is a region known as the "Banana Belt." Many people think that the Banana Belt is a feature unique to the Finger Lakes. They are mistaken. The term Banana Belt can be found in Merriam-Webster and defined as, "any segment of a larger geographic region that enjoys warmer weather conditions than the region as a whole, especially in the wintertime."

Think of a small "belt" of land that possesses warmer (tropical) conditions. It's likely that when you think of the places where bananas grow, you think of a warm, tropical region. There are "banana belts" in Colorado, Idaho, Montana, Arkansas, and around the globe. No, you can't grow bananas in those areas, but bananas grow in warm regions; the belts are small tracts of land—thus the name.

Winter temperatures in the Finger Lakes can often reach -20°F. Seneca Lake last froze completely in 1912, as it did again in 1855, 1875, and 1885. The lake has not frozen in well over 100 years. The deepest part of Seneca Lake is opposite Wagner Vineyards' 225 acres of grapes. A prevailing wind blows out of the northwest nearly constantly. It blows across Seneca Lake (which can be as much as 50° warmer than the prevailing winter temperatures) before reaching Wagner Vineyards. That wind blowing across a warmer body of water will cause the land mass near the lake to be warmer—thus, a "banana belt." Some consider that territory to be the finest growing region in the Finger Lakes.

Air on flat ground is stagnant. In warmer climates, grapes typically bud into tiny flowers in mid-March. In the Finger Lakes, if grapes bud this early, and there is a frost, there will be no crop that year. In the Finger Lakes, with the steep sides surrounding the lakes, air is in constant motion, rolling downhill, bouncing off a very cold lake in the spring and being pushed back uphill to keep the vineyards cool and delaying the "bud break."

Bud break occurs at the end of April and into May, when frost is less likely. In the fall, during the October and early November months of harvest, the air rolls down the hill, and the northwest wind blows across a lake that is still warm from the summer months. This keeps the vineyards warm and free from a crippling frost. For most of my life (so far), I lived 20 miles south of Wagner Vineyards. My home was on flat land away from Seneca Lake. I often lost my flower gardens to an October frost, while the grapes at Wagner's were fine, thanks to the microclimate created by Seneca Lake.

The Syracuse and Rochester regions of upstate New York are less than 80 miles from the heart of the Finger Lakes. Both regions are known for their extreme winter cold and heavy snow storms. Upstate New York has a macroclimate of extreme winter cold and snowfall. Remember, the microclimate is the climate within a macroclimate. It is the climate of a very small or restricted area that differs from the climate in the surrounding area.

The microclimate of the Finger Lakes is the perfect example of microclimate. The individual elements of the terroir of the Finger Lakes combine to make this region a world class wine destination.

Appendix III: Minerality

It is almost impossible to read any description of the taste of a Riesling without encountering this author's much-despised term, "minerality." When speaking with my Wagner customers, I never use words or phrases that I think they will not understand. Minerality is one of those words. If you take a few minutes to look for the word on the internet, you will find something like this:

There is really no agreement among wine experts or even wine scientists as to how to define minerality in a wine. Some tasters compare it to the smell or taste of wet stones, crushed rocks, salinity, a flintiness, or even a savory earthiness. In contrast, the scientific community tends to refer more to the volatile substances in wine such as sulphur or *fusel* compounds. (Fusel refers to excessive concentrations of some alcohols that may cause off-flavors that are sometimes described as spicy, hot, or solvent-like.)

Others think of minerality in terms of minerals in the soil that might end up in a wine. Soils contain varying amounts of potassium, nitrogen, phosphorus, sulfur, magnesium, calcium, and iron. However, opinions differ as to whether the grapes—and the resulting wine—actually absorb any of these minerals from the soil. Soils that are alive and healthy supposedly are capable of transferring more minerals to the plant. Research and opinion are still somewhat divided, however.

Let's start with what is known: The International Mineralogical Association defines "mineral" as, "an element or chemical compound that is normally crystalline and that has been formed as a result of geological processes."

So, should we assume that vines soak up elements from the soil, lending their distinct flavors to the grapes and, therefore, the wine? Not really. The mineral elements in wine are tiny; only potassium and calcium even come close to 1,000 parts per million. Scientists do not believe that you can taste them.

Wine blogger, Mary Gorman-McAdams writes:

> *One of the most difficult questions to answer, and one of the most divisive is whether you can actually taste minerality, and if so what does it taste like. Is it really a taste or more of a sensation? Can you actually smell and taste stones or rocks? I would argue yes. Wines that have obvious minerality tend to make you salivate, not because of the wine's acidity, but more of a savory and non-fruit evoked salivation. However, sensations of minerality are delicate and more nuanced, that can be easily overpowered by overt fruitiness or oak in a wine.*

So, after pouring more wine than anyone else at Wagner Vineyards during my 4+ years in residence, my observations have been that the general wine tasting public has no idea what "minerality" means. Join the club!

I have recently been using the pH scale in explaining the acidity in the Wagner Rieslings. (See the article on acidity in Appendix IV.) I explain the scale, then I pour samples to show how sugar hides acidity.

The term minerality was first used in the early 1980s. No one—*and I mean no one*—has a definitive definition that all wine people can agree on. But, if you read any explanation of the taste of a Riesling, you will encounter the word minerality. So, in the immortal words of Supreme Court Justice Potter Stewart, in a 1964 case to determine the definition of "obscenity," which is not protected by the First Amendment, when it comes to minerality, "I will know it when I see it." I believe that the same can be said for a Riesling that has significant "minerality." You have all been in the woods and smelled wet rocks and shale rocks. You can get that smell ("nose") from certain Rieslings. "You will know it when you smell it."

Appendix IV: Acids in Wine

Grab a fresh lemon. Cut it in half. Take a deep bite. Before you even bit into it, you already knew the sensation that you would experience, didn't you? Lemon juice contains high levels of acid, thus it is acidic. Those of us with developing palates have often heard about the "acidity" in the wine that we are sampling. Biting the lemon is, of course, one of the highest levels of tasting acid.

Lemon has acid. Grapes have acid. Wine has acid. Regulating the acid in the finished product—the bottle of wine—is one of the most important tasks in winemaking. The acid affects the color, the balance, and the taste of wine. The total amount of acid in a wine is measured in terms of pH. (pH is a measure of acidity, from 0 to 7). The pH number is an indicator of how acidic a substance is. The greater the acidity, the lower the pH value. Alkaline is the opposite of acid. Alkaline solutions have a higher pH value, measured from 7 to 14. Substances that aren't acidic or alkaline are considered *neutral* solutions; they usually have a pH of 7. In theory, water is a neutral solution and should have a pH of 7, but with phenomena such as Acid Rain, and other environmental factors that can affect water, even good old water is not necessarily "neutral."

When we were young, we learned that, to make a fire, the necessary elements are oxygen, heat, and fuel. The necessary elements of wine are alcohol, sweetness, tannin, and acid. And to confuse you a bit more, there are many different types of acid in a wine that will affect how tart and sour it tastes.

In wine tasting, the term "acidity" refers to the fresh, tart and sour attributes of the wine which are evaluated in relation to how well the acidity balances out the sweet and bitter components of the wine. There are three different types of acid in wine: tartaric, citric, and malic. Remember that low pH means high acid. Worldwide, the pH of wine typically ranges from 2.5 to 4.5 pH. Finger Lakes wines range from 2.8 to 4. (For comparison, keep these pH values in mind: Pepsi Cola, 2.5; lemonade, 2.6; red and white wines, 3.5; low acid red wines, 4.0; coffee, 4.5, and milk, 6.7) The numbers assigned for pH are orders of magnitude. Therefore, wine with a pH of 3 is *ten times* as acidic as a wine with a pH of 4.

Remember how you anticipate the "tart and sour" taste of biting into that lemon. Now, try to transfer that to the taste of wine—mostly white wines, and most assuredly Riesling, the staple of the Finger Lakes, considered by many to be the most acidic of wines. Consider the fact that sweetness lowers the sensation of acidity. Squeeze the other half of that fresh lemon in a glass and taste it. Then take a drink of Pepsi. They have the same pH (about 2.5), but the Pepsi has high sugar content. Rieslings are labeled as dry, semi-dry, and sweet. Notice the difference on your tongue as the wines get sweeter and sweeter. The acidity is technically the same, but it doesn't "taste" the same because of the higher levels of (residual) sugar.

Appendix V: Malolactic Fermentation

Grapes contain citric, tartaric, and malic acids. Before describing this type of fermentation, it might be useful to give a quick background of the two acids involved:

Malic acid contributes to the pleasantly sour taste of fruits and was first identified in unripe apples by Swedish pharmacist Carl Wilhelm Schelle in 1785. The word "malic" is derived from the Latin word for apple, "malum," which is why this particular acid is closely associated with its namesake fruit.

Lactic acid was first isolated from sour milk by Scheele five years earlier, in 1780. The term reflects the lact-combining form derived from the Latin word for milk. Lactic acid is found primarily in sour milk products, such as yogurt and buttermilk.

Once in awhile, a more knowledgeable wine drinker will ask if our Chardonnays have gone through a "malolactic fermentation" process. At Wagner Vineyards, the answer will be no. If, however, they ask about our red wines, the answer is yes. All of the Wagner red wines go through this second fermentation. Put very simply, malolactic fermentation removes the malic acid from the wine, leaving it with the impression of smoothness, even butteriness (more in whites like Chardonnays, but not so much in reds). Malic acid occurs naturally in wine grapes. It has a sharp, tart taste. Some people compare it to the taste of a green apple that has not fully ripened. That tart taste enhances the taste of our Riesling wines, which really are not usual candidates for this type of fermentation. In the 1970s, southern California winemakers began to soften the taste of tart Chardonnays with the process of malolactic fermentation, thus the question from that sophisticated wine drinker. Malolactic fermentation gives Chardonnays a smoother, buttery finish, that is further enhanced by spending time in an oak barrel.

Many of our Finger Lakes neighbors use this second fermentation process for their Chardonnays, and then finish them in oak barrels. Wagner Vineyards does not use malolactic fermentation for our Reserve or Barrel Fermented Chardonnays because it is simply not necessary. Wagner Vineyards Chardonnay grapes are grown in such a way that they do not require a second fermentation to lower the grapes' acid. The longer a grape remains on the vine, the more sugar it gains and the less acid it becomes.

The grape "canopy" includes the trunk, stems, leaves, and fruit of a grapevine. A trellis system arranges or spreads out the stems, leaves and fruit so sunlight can help them grow and flourish. Different trellis systems spread the canopy in different ways. The Scott-Henry Trellis System used by Wagner's enables the grape canopy to increase sugar and decrease acid throughout the October harvest. For the terroir in the Finger Lakes Region, John Wagner feels that the Scott-Henry System is the best.

The taste of acid in red wines is *not* desirable. Malolactic fermentation allows us to remove the acid taste in our red wines, before the wine is transferred to our oak barrels.

This second fermentation, often referred to as "malo" (or MLF) uses special bacteria (oenococcus oeni) to convert the tart malic acid into the smoother lactic acid by using special bacteria. When you see our Vinifera red wines in the fermentation tanks in November, they will be experiencing a "malo" fermentation, after which they will spend more than a year in oak barrels in the wine cellar. Those red wines will have already been experiencing the effects of the magical single-celled fungus known as yeast, which changes their sugars to alcohol and carbon dioxide. The above named bacteria, oenococcus oeni, is added to the tank to convert the tart malic acid to a smoother lactic acid.

A malolactic fermentation can reduce the acid in a wine from 0.1 to 0.3 percent. That may not sound like a lot, but it is noticeable on one's palate. The wine seems "softer," lacking the acidic bite. In oaked Chardonnays and in red wines, this allows the fruit flavors to mesh with the oak resulting in the taste that red wine lovers crave.

To put it simply, all grapes have acid. All grapes have malic acid. You should expect a tart finish when tasting our highly acclaimed Caywood East Riesling. You do *not* expect that same finish with our Pinot Noir Reserve, which is, in my humble opinion, quite possibly the best Pinot in our region. Malolactic fermentation, which converts the acid in the grapes, is largely responsible for the smooth finish of our red wines.

Appendix VI: Barrel Selection

This appendix is *not* intended to be a scientific discussion of how oak imparts such an "artful" taste to the barreled wines that we drink. I won't undertake a scientific explanation of how the cell walls of oak (cellulose) impart certain taste to the wine. I will leave it to an expert, Daniel Pambianch, who wrote in Oak Barrel Chemistry, in 2011: "Cellulose is a very large polymer of glucose where the high number of hydroxyl groups can form many hydrogen bonds (with adjacent oxygen-containing molecules) to give wood its structural strength. Hemicellulose is a shorter polymer of glucose and many different sugar monomers form hydrogen bonds with cellulose. And lignin fills the spaces in the cell wall between cellulose, hemicellulose and pectin components."

In simpler, more readable English, I intend to explain why using oak in aging and fermenting wine is really an art form.

It is thought that the first barrels were created by the Celtic tribes—Whales, Scotland, Ireland, England—over 2000 years ago. Before they were replaced by plastic, cardboard, and metal, barrels were used to carry everything from nails to gunpowder, salted meats and fish, animal hides, cement, coconut oil, cornmeal, flour, sugar, pickles, potatoes, and of course, beer, whiskey, and wine. The majority of the world's barrels today are used to ferment, age, and impart a unique taste to whiskey and wine.

French and American white oak are "artfully" used in creating the world's great wines. French oak is known for contributing subtle overtones of vanilla and spices, while American oak generally has more pronounced flavors of coconut and vanilla, which can be toned down if the oak is allowed to dry out for an extra year of drying time. French oak trees are generally harvested when they are 150 years old. American oak is usually just 60 years old. When an oak tree is cut, the moisture level of the wood is between 50 and 80 percent. Before a barrel-maker (or "cooper") can begin to craft a barrel, the moisture level in French oak must be 14%; American oak is crafted at 12%.

After the tree is felled, it is cut into log bolts, typically one foot by four feet, and stacked outside. The best way to dry the freshly cut oak that will be used for wine and whiskey barrels is to air dry the pieces outside, regardless of regional weather. Fungi penetrate the moist wood and draw out the flavors coveted by winemakers. During this air drying process the moisture evaporates from both within and between the wood cells. Sun and wind speed up the process, while snow and rain slow it. Rain washes away the harsh tannin that has been leached out by the fungi and the drying process. This softens the wood flavors.

Barrels can be sufficiently air dried in two years. American oak seems to have more pronounced tannin levels than French oak, and therefore can benefit from a third year of aging. Once dried to the cooper's liking, the bolts must be cut into the "staves" that form the actual barrel. Because American oak is denser than French oak, it can be sawed. French oak must be hand split along the grain of the wood to prevent leaking. Hand splitting yields a smaller amount of usable wood; therefore, French barrels are much more costly.

Barrels are curved, but the newly cut staves are straight. The staves must be bent or shaped. If you have ever tried to bend a short oak board, you will understand why the oak staves must be heated to soften the oak in preparation for bending it.

Water and fire can be used to soften the oak for barrel shaping. After being shaped by both water and fire, the barrels that will be used for wine are further toasted. (Whiskey barrels are charred instead.) Toasting both mellows the tannin in the wood and changes the flavors the barrel impart, from raw wood to more spicy, vanilla notes that barrels are known to pass on to the wine that is aged within. The beloved vanilla taste comes from the cellulose of the oak in the form of an organic compound known as vanillin. The toasting process releases the vanillin from the cellulose of the wood.

Water bending is the gentlest method. It is also the newer method employed to soften oak for bending. Wagner Vineyards acquires many of their barrels from Barrel Associates of Napa, California. Barrel

Associates has been using the water bent method for over 20 years. They borrowed this water bending technique from Dargaud & Jaegle of Burgundy, France. The Jaegle family has been developing and perfecting this process for nearly a century. During the forming process, the newly shaped barrel is immersed in boiling water. At this temperature, very little caramelization of the wood occurs. The sugars will begin to caramelize at about 160°C. Eric Mercier, President of Barrel Associates, told me that by boiling the "shell," you extract some of the harsher tannin from the oak, and you are able to toast the oak deeper without burning the inside of the barrel, due to the fact that water is a better conductor of heat than air. You therefore develop different flavor profiles.

Fire bending, the most common method in barrel production worldwide, is a much more extreme than water bending. The inside surface, which is directly exposed to the fire, becomes so hot that it caramelizes the sugars. Fire bending also breaks down tannin at a far greater rate than the water bent staves.

Let me repeat: winemaking is an art form. If you give 10 artists a canvas and an identical palette of paints, and instruct them to paint Seneca Lake, you will get 10 different interpretations. If you walk into an art gallery to buy a painting for your home, you will find paintings you love and paintings you would never put on your walls. What makes you choose one vs. the other? Maybe the red that appeals to you in one artist's palette is the fire bent barrel. Perhaps the pink in another is the water bent barrel. Which "color" should our winemaker use? If you ask 10 winemakers to create a Chardonnay from the 20 barrels that are composed of old and new oak, water bent and fire bent oak, the result will be 10 different interpretations of barrel fermented Chardonnay. Just as you discovered in the art shop, you will love some of the interpretations, while determining that others don't belong on your wall (or your table).

Eric Mercier says that water bent barrels tend to be more "respectful" of the fruit, while adding a little more weight in the mid-palate. (Mid-palate is the taste you get between your first impression when the wine hits your mouth and the point when you swallow.) This is the part of tasting where the wine coats your taste buds to leave the impression of sweet or sour or savory or bitter.

Water bent barrels are more often used for white wines and lighter reds. Fire bent barrels are slowly softened over an open fire built from scraps of the same oak that comprises the barrel. This imparts a rich and balanced to the typically red wine.

According to Barrel Associates, water bent barrels "help to elevate fruit aromas and provide structure to your wine with sweet, toasty oak flavors and great palate length. Fire bent barrels provide an extra lift of oak and an enhanced aromatic profile."

Barrel Associates concludes that the choice of the two differently treated barrels "offers a 'spice rack' that enables winemakers to select from a broad palette. Particular fruit qualities and stylistic objectives might call for a fire bent barrel, to add structure, a dominant spice or an assertive finish. An especially juicy, jammy lot might be better showcased by the nuances of a water bent barrel."

Appendix VII: Tasting Tannin

Unless you drink exclusively white wine, it would be almost impossible to explore a wine region without hearing about tannin. But once you cross into oaked Chardonnay and red wine territory, someone will definitely mention "tannin."

What is tannin? Why does the mouth interpret the "finish" of red wines differently from that of whites? Why does a Cabernet Franc Rosé finish so differently from a classic Cabernet Franc? The answer: tannin. (Tannin is a chemical compound, which gives wine structure, and naturally comes from the grapes' skins, seeds and stems.)

First, let's discuss where the word tannin comes from. You've probably heard the Christmas song, "O Tannenbaum," an old German Christmas carol about a Christmas tree. "Tannenbaum" is German for fir tree. Somehow "the ancients" found that using the ground up bark from a tree (especially an oak tree, not a fir tree, as was first used) helped in the process of curing leather. Thus, the term for turning animal hides into leather using powdered tree bark, turning the hides a *tan* color, became known as tanning and the ground up bark known as tannin.

After the bark was removed, it was placed on the ground with the inner—or flesh—side facing up to hasten drying and prevent formation of mold. Bark was then stacked in large piles off the ground to dry further while awaiting transport to the tannery.

At the tannery, conveniently located on rivers or lakes, the bark was ground or shredded before being placed in tubs filled with hot water. Using a passive method, it took about four days for the tannin to leach out of the bark; steam infusions cut that time in half. The resulting tanning liquor was circulated through tanning vats containing increasingly acidic solutions. Spent bark was then dried for fuel to heat the vats. (Hugh Canham, Hemlock and Hide: The Tanbark Industry in Old New York.)

We've established the origins of the term, tannin. Now you understand why tannin is found in (red) wines. It is also found in tea, cocoa, chocolate, coffee, some herbal preparations, grapes, and certain fruits, including blackberries and cranberries.

We still don't completely understand the properties of tannin, but there have been countless studies that show that people who consume red wine, tea, cocoa, chocolate (and the rest) have fewer cavities, less diarrhea, and much lower incidence of heart disease and cancer. Tannin has also been reported to exert other physiological effects, such as to accelerate blood clotting, reduce blood pressure, decrease the serum lipid level, prevent liver necrosis, and modulate immune responses. Tannin disables bacteria in the mouth, which inhibits plaque formation. Tooth decay is also decreased. (Unfortunately, it has also been shown that drinking red wine will stain your healthier, relatively cavity-free teeth.)

The power of tannin comes mainly from its astringent properties. (Astringency creates the sensation we describe as making your mouth "pucker.") This happens when the tannin attaches to the proteins in saliva, creating a rough sensation in the mouth, resulting in a dry, chalky, wrinkling, tightening sensation.

Finally, try this: Pour a small tasting of our Cabernet Franc Rosé. Remember, the juice of a red grape is basically white. If you crush Cabernet Franc grapes as soon as you harvest them, you will have white wine. We bring the grapes into our warehouse and manually crush the skins into the juice, two or three times a day, for about a week. The juice sitting on the skins turns red and the tannin from the skins is absorbed into the juice. That juice will eventually be aged in oak barrels for over a year.

Our Rosé spends about 12 hours on the skins and zero time in oak. It is literally the white wine of a red grape, thus the total absence of tannin. Taste our Rosé. It "finishes" fruity—some people (like me) taste strawberries.

Now try the classic Cabernet Franc—one week on the skins, more than a year in oak, and lots of tannin. As you taste the red wine, you may taste the Rosé during the split second when it first hits your tongue. Then the oak taste will kick in as the wine passes your tongue; then, you will feel a dry, bitter, tightening sensation. You have just "tasted tannin."

Appendix VIII: Bottle Shock

"Bottle shock" and "bottle sickness" are terms used in many publications to describe a condition in a wine where its desired flavors are temporarily altered or jumbled.

There are two main scenarios in which bottle shock sets in: First, the wine is "shocked" at being transferred into a new environment (the glass bottle) from the environment to which it was accustomed (the tank) as it passes through several filters on its path to the bottle. Some people might describe the wine as "becoming shy in its new environment, retreating into itself, tightening up, even acting sour for a few days or weeks before settling down and remembering its true self"—the way it tasted from the tank before it was bottled.

I recently moved my cat into a new environment. She has lived with me for three plus years, where she had the run of the house and had no other animals or humans to contend with. I moved her into a new house with another human and 5 other cats. She retreated into herself, tightening up, acting sour (mean) before she settled down, remembering that she liked having the run of the house, not living under the bed. The second scenario of bottle shock occurs when wines —especially fragile older wines—are shaken in travel, perhaps across an ocean or cross-country. The wine will often experience the same "bottle shock," as their original taste becomes "altered or jumbled."

Few people know that the negative impact of bottle shock on red wine is the reason that the favorite wine on the Titanic was white— particularly Champagne. Red wines, like Cabernet Sauvignon, were not well-regarded in that environment because they experienced "bottle shock" from being stored in the ship's hold, constantly shaken by the ocean travel. (Modern wine-production employs sophisticated filtering techniques that help mitigate the bottle shock factor.)

It is thought that a wine's complex elements (phenolics, tannin and other compounds) constantly evolve, both on their own and in relation to each other. Heat or motion can add stress to this evolution, causing the process of continued development of the wine to shut down temporarily. The wine won't taste like the flavors are melding together in the way they should. The jostling that the wine undergoes (from leaving the tank or on a long trip) can actually cause these elements to get out of sync. The wine isn't corked or oxidized, it just seems flat. It lacks both the fruitiness and its character. If you open a bottle of "shocked" wine it will improve after a day or two. Your other bottles of the same wine will be fine after they've had a chance to settle. No one really knows what causes this phenomenon, but since it happens whenever a great tasting wine leaves the tank and enters the bottle (or a previously-bottled wine travels a great distance), bottle shock is a real thing.

There is a theory that bottle shock occurs when the wine absorbs too much oxygen in too little time. That is likely to happen during bottling, though we try very hard to prevent it. It can also happen during shipping. Constant temperature changes and the sloshing of the wine in the bottle allows more air to pass through the cork than would normally occur.

Wines can handle the slow, gradual infusion of air that occurs naturally through wine corks. In fact, most red wines will actually benefit from such a scenario, but when the oxygen infiltrates too fast, there is a build-up of an element called acetaldehyde.

I have constantly written that I do not like to get too technical in this book or in any of my writings, but "acetaldehyde" comes up quite often in my research of "bottle shock."

According to Wineland Media, June 2015:

Acetaldehyde (ethanal, C_2H_4O) is a low molecular weight, flavour compound found in a wide variety of aromatic foods and beverages that have, prior to their final stage of production, undergone a degree of fermentation. For almost a hundred years, acetaldehyde has been known to be a product of alcoholic fermentation by yeasts, but its presence in wine was not confirmed until 1984, by Dittrich and Barth. It is one of the most important aldehydes *(carbonyl compounds) and constitutes more than 90% of the total aldehyde content in wine. Aldehydes, together with a number of other volatile compounds, are responsible for wine aroma.*

Acetaldehyde is primarily a product of yeast metabolism of sugars during the first stages of alcoholic fermentation. It is the last precursor in yeast fermentation before ethanol is formed, and is produced when pyruvate, the end product of glycolysis, is converted by the enzyme, alcohol dehydrogenase (ADH), to acetaldehyde. Conversely, a secondary source of acetaldehyde production in red wine, which usually occurs after ageing, is oxidation (exposure to air / oxygen) of ethanol, once again facilitated by the enzyme, alcohol dehydrogenase.

Acetaldehyde is naturally found in any wine, at least in small, unnoticeable amounts. In higher amounts, its presence can be detected as an odor of nuts. This is what's noticed in wines that are suffering from bottle shock. The normal chain of events that occurs during aging is disrupted by the production of an abundance of acetaldehyde.

Over the course of time, the acetaldehyde will slowly convert to alcohol, bringing the wine back into line with something enjoyable to drink. How long this takes depends on the severity of the bottle shock. It could be as little as a few days or as long as a few weeks.

No one really knows why "bottle shock" happens. And other than introducing the concept of acetaldehyde, I have tried to keep this as simple as possible. Bottle shock is real, and we must deal with it. I might also suggest that if you are a member of a wine club and some of the bottles in your shipment are ten years old or older, especially if they are red, you should wait a few weeks before you open them. Now you know why bottle shock occurs.

Appendix IX: Noble Rot/Botrytis Cinerea

Noble Rot or botrytis cinerea is a *good* fungus that shrivels and decays wine grapes. The same type of fungus produces penicillin, Stilton blue cheese, and, unfortunately, athlete's foot. Botrytis cinerea can occur on fruits, vegetables and flowers. That moldy strawberry at the bottom of the carton is "noble rot." While it can be very beneficial to specific types of grapes—typically white grapes and the very sweet wines they produce—it can be devastating to red grapes, especially Pinot Noir.

Infestation by botrytis requires a specific set of climatic conditions: humidity, rain, and morning dew, followed by very dry afternoon heat. Botrytis attacks ripe, thin-skinned grapes. If the weather stays wet, the damage from "gray rot" (or bunch rot), the evil twin of "noble" rot, can destroy entire crops of grapes.

The "rot" normally occurs when the grapes are ripe and ready for harvest. When the dampness occurs, the "rot" forms and penetrates the skins of the grapes, evaporating the water inside the grape and leaving behind the sugar as the grape begins to dry. The grapes take on the appearance of raisins. (Destructive gray rot develops when the botrytis causes the grape to split open rather than shrivel, allowing other fungal and bacterial infections to take hold.)

If you enjoy sweet wines, the grapes infected with noble—not gray— rot produce delicious and very concentrated, unique sweet wines. These "botrytized" wines date to the 1630s. Because they know a whole lot more than I do, and because I could actually understand this, I share with you a 2016 article from Cornell University's Viticulture and Enology Program, written by Wayne Wilcox:

> Botrytis bunch rot (BBR), caused by the fungus botrytis cinerea, causes damage to ripening grape clusters throughout the temperate regions of the world where pre-harvest rains occur. Although pure botrytis infections

free of secondary contaminants can sometimes produce the so-called 'noble rot' integral to the production of certain prized dessert wines, a far more common result is a disease that reduces both yield and fruit quality, as infected grapes typically produce wines with substandard flavors and appearance. BBR is an amazingly complex disease. Its development is governed by multiple 3-way interactions between the grapevine, the environment, and the botrytis fungus itself, many of which are poorly understood.

About ten years ago a good friend who works at a local winery asked me to help hand-pick Pinot Noir grapes that were infested with botrytis bunch rot. It was not a pleasant day. Yes, Pinot Noir is a very thin-skinned grape. It grows in very tight clusters and is considered to be one of the most difficult grapes to grow because of these factors.

When I was asked to help hand-pick the Pinot Noir grapes, it had rained steadily for two days. The grapes were to be harvested on Monday and it rained. The rot began almost immediately. Then it rained and rained. By Wednesday, the rot was visible on every cluster. Armed with a pair of scissors and plastic gloves, I was instructed to cut off a cluster, then rub off the rot with my gloved fingers. The rot fell easily from the clusters. It was a very hot day and it seemed like there were more bees than good grapes. Never again!

You might ask if there are steps that can be taken to minimize or protect a vineyard from "gray rot." There are. Good canopy management practices allow air flow and fungicide spray coverage to the grape clusters, starting early in the growing season.

According to the Oregon State University Extension Service, September 12, 2018:

These canopy practices must be appropriately timed during vine growth (bloom time or later) and should be used in vineyards with moderate to high vegetative vigor. One of the most effective canopy management practices is cluster zone leaf removal on the morning-sun side of the canopy early in the season to ensure maximum benefit, particularly in cool climate production regions. Leaf removal should be conducted on vines where you cannot see the clusters and should be done any time from just before bloom to just after fruit set.

The second step in prevention is the use of well-timed fungicide applications, targeting applications to the cluster zone at bloom and just prior to bunch closure. Fungicides may need to be applied before rain events post-veraison to prevent conditions that may lead to infection.

There is a very fine line between a botrytis "noble rot" and a botrytis "bunch rot." Climatic conditions can and will control the outcome of either. Proper preparation of the vineyard and proper vineyard practices can help mitigate potential damage.

Appendix X: Clones & Mutations

CLONES

I had a problem understanding the concept of grape clones and how they differ from mutations. I'll try to break it down.

Let's go back to the Bible and the story of creation—Adam and Eve, followed by all the rest of us. There are many ancient grapes, but let's break them down to Gouais Blanc, Savagnin, and, of course, Pinot Noir. They are the grape equivalents of Adam and Eve (plus a few friends) of modern grapes. Most grape varietals can trace their DNA structure back to those three grapes.(A varietal wine is a wine made primarily from a single named grape variety, and which typically displays the name of that variety on the wine label. Examples of grape varieties commonly used in varietal wines are Riesling, Cabernet Sauvignon, Chardonnay and Merlot.)

It was reported in the news more than 20 years ago that scientists were attempting to clone certain animals. On July 5, 1996, Dolly the Sheep was born in a lab in Scotland. No, the ewe did not give birth to Dolly in a lab. Scientist had taken DNA from an adult sheep's mammary gland and used it to create another sheep. Dolly was the first "cloned" animal.

A simple definition for clone would be a copy or imitation of something already existing. A definition more suitable for this discussion would be that a clone is the "aggregate of genetically identical cells or organisms asexually produced by or from a single progenitor cell or organism." (No, that's not my definition. I am not a science student—at least not anymore. That is Mr. Webster's definition and one of many that you can find.

Before really getting into what I think a clone is, let's discuss what it is *not*. A clone is not a "cross." The example of a cross that I use most often is the world's number one planted grape, Cabernet Sauvignon. In the late 1600s, a bee (or perhaps the wind) touched the male part of the flower of the Sauvignon Blanc grape and flew over to touch the female part of the Cabernet Franc grape's flower. Cabernet Sauvignon was their love-child. This was an entirely new, totally different grape. It was a cross of Sauvignon Blanc and Cabernet Franc. It was not a clone. A clone is very different from a cross (or hybrid). Our Cayuga White is a Cornell grape, created in a lab from the French hybrid, Seyval Blanc, and the New York hybrid, Schuyler. These are manmade hybrids that resulted in an entirely new grape.

Clones, on the other hand, are variations of a single grape. Different clones of a Riesling may have more sugar, or less acid, or greater disease resistance, or larger clusters.

Grapes are planted by using a piece of the "mother vine" grafted to root stock suitable for growing in the climate and soil of different regions. With only one parent, the genetic makeup of the new vine *should* be the same. But no...

There are billions of cells in every grapevine. So let's say that a new Cabernet Franc vineyard is planted with a thousand vines. The "mother" vine is the part that is planted in the ground. It is not the shoots that come from it. After 10 years, the vineyard master notices that one of the vines is producing many more clusters of grapes than all of the other vines. The clusters seem to hang closer to the ground and the grapes are a little darker, the juice seems slightly different, and mildew does not seem to form when it rains. He gives cuttings to a scientist friend at a nearby university, who plants many of the cuttings, waits 3 or 4 years for the vines to produce grapes and finds that they are definitely genetically different from the other 999 vines in the vineyard. This is a new clone of the Cabernet grape and it is given a number and perhaps named after the vineyard master.

Let's say that an established winery like Wagner Vineyards is going to plant a new Cabernet Franc vineyard. Their original Cabernet Franc vineyard is more than 25 years old. With so much new information and so many different clones of Cabernet Franc, John Wagner can study information about the various clones and may even call other vineyard masters who have used them. Many factors go into choosing the right clone. In 2016, wine writer John Poplin wrote:

> The vineyard master and winemaker may look to specific clones to achieve the end result that they are looking for in a wine. Some grape clones may be more fruit forward while others offer more structure. Some clones may have higher sugars or acidity, which can alter a wine's alcohol content or create a more crisp and refreshing wine. Some may simply grow better in a specific region, in regards to climate or soil type. So when selecting grape clones, the winemaker or vineyard master has the ability to already steer their wines in a specific direction.

MUTATIONS

So, what about a grape mutation? I think the easiest way to see the difference is to look at the Pinot Noir grape. The most obvious mutations are mutations of color. Pinot Noir has mutated over the centuries into Pinot Gris and Pinot Blanc.

Young clones seem to be more susceptible to mutations than older clones. The vines react to the environment differently. It is the plants' way of adapting to its surroundings: sun, soil, rain and more. Mutations are caused by a slight genetic variation in the billions of cells of a grapevine. As a result, the new vine will no longer be identical to the parent vine. Not all mutations are favorable, but in the case of Pinot Noir to Pinot Gris to Pinot Blanc the resulting wines are very favorable indeed.

Researchers at the University of California at Davis, have determined that Pinot Gris has a remarkably similar DNA profile to Pinot Noir and that the color difference is derived from a genetic mutation that occurred centuries ago. The leaves and the vines of both grapes are so similar that coloration is the only thing that differentiates the two.

Pinot Gris is today a world popular white grape. The vast majority of white grapes have green skins. When Pinot Noir mutated to Pinot Gris, the redness of its skin compelled wine makers to make red wine.

When they realized that the red wine made from these lighter colored red skins was not good, they tried making white wine from these grapes. Pinto Gris (Grigio) is now the 4th most popular white wine in the world.

Pinot Blanc appeared much later, as a mutation of Pino Gris, first noticed in the early Middle Ages. It is often mistaken for Chardonnay

So, in the simplest of terms, if you look at a clone of a mother vine, you probably cannot tell the difference. If you look at a *mutation* of a mother vine, the difference is (usually) in full view. On the vine, Pinot Noir is a dark black color, Pinot Gris is dark gray, and Pinot Blanc is the traditional green of a white grape. In a lab, the DNA makeup of the 3 grapes is incredibly similar. In a glass, the three grapes translate to 3 distinct wines.

Appendix XI: Residual Sugar

A wine's sweetness vs. dryness is probably the most rudimentary lesson for the novice wine drinker. Does the wine contain a lot of sugar (is it sweet) or is there very little to no sugar, which would be termed "dry"?

Most wine consumers don't realize that there are three acids in every grape. Nor do they understand the effects of cold storage or cold stabilization, or the impact of sulfites. But, even if they aren't familiar with the specific term, the vast majority *do* know something about "residual sugar" (RS), the amount of sugar that remains in a wine after the fermentation process is complete.

In whiskey- and beer-making, the starches in the grains are converted to sugars before fermentation can begin. In winemaking, the juice from the grape contains a large amount sugar. Live yeast is added to the juice, where it feasts on the sugar, like kids on Halloween. As the yeast consumes the sugar in the juice, it produces three things; alcohol, carbon dioxide gas (CO_2), and heat. The alcohol is our objective; the CO_2 is vented off; the heat generated by the fermentation is controlled by the cooling jackets that are wrapped around the fermenting tanks or by the process of manual punch-downs of the red fermenter caps several times a day. Any sugar that is left over, deliberately or not, is called residual sugar. It is the measure of sugar solids that remain unfermented in a finished wine, or any sugar that might be added when making a very sweet wine.

Residual sugar concentration is expressed in grams per litre (g/L) or as a percentage of weight to volume. For example: a wine with 0.4% residual sugar, like the Wagner 2018 Caywood East, contains four grams of sugar in every litre of the wine. The main fermentable sugars in grape juice are glucose and fructose. Although each type of sugar exists in approximately equal concentrations in wine, fructose is roughly twice as sweet as glucose. Glucose is also fermented at a faster rate, which means that a wine fermented to dryness will have less residual glucose than fructose. Any glucose and fructose sugars remaining in the wine at the end of fermentation contribute to residual sugar. Even if two wines have the same residual sugar concentration, the one with more fructose will taste sweeter.

The fermentation process also relies on temperature. The warmer the juice is, the faster the sugars are converted to alcohol. Conversely, the cooler the juice, the slower the process. If you've ever made bread, you probably remember that when the dough has been mixed, it is never placed first in a refrigerator. Instead, you find a warm place in the house for the yeast to react to the flour to make it "rise."

Yeast likes being warm. If the winemaker chills the juice (now wine) sufficiently, fermentation will stop; the yeast is discarded and, therefore, no more fermentation occurs. If there is sugar left over, you have a sweeter wine.

Fermentation may stop for other reasons, too. The age-old method has to do with the amount of alcohol remaining in the wine after fermentation. Different strains of yeast tolerate different levels of alcohol. A weaker strain of yeast might die off before it consumes all the sugar in the fermenting wine.

Not only does leftover or residual sugar (RS) have a sweetening effect on the taste of wine, it can also help white wines to age well. White wines with a little sugar seem to age better than those without. The wine seems to evolve, the sugar compounds change shape, and the taste of the wine seems to dry out a bit.

The relative sweetness of a wine is also affected by factors such as the levels of acidity and alcohol, the amount of tannin, and whether or not the wine is sparkling. A sweet wine, such as a Riesling, may actually taste dry due to the high level of acidity. Conversely, a dry wine may taste sweet if the alcohol level is elevated.

In wine, sugar and acid are on the opposite sides of the "balancing act" of a good wine. If the winemaker leaves some sugar, the wine probably has strong acid. In a wine like our beloved Riesling, which is a classic high-acid wine, a little RS can greatly enhance the taste.

The word "cloying" is often used in the description of the Wagner Riesling Ice Wine. It is a term that many of our customers ask us to define. Cloying simply means "an excess of sweetness," or simply too sweet. So a wine that is "without being cloying" would be sweet, but not sickeningly sweet. Such "balanced" wines avoid the cloying taste associated with elevated levels of sugar by carefully utilizing the natural acidity in the grapes. This means that the finest sweet wines are made with grape varietals that retain their acidity, even at very high ripeness levels, such as Riesling, Chenin Blanc, and Sauvignon Blanc. Both of the Wagner dry Rieslings have a touch of sugar (.6% and .4%), while all three of the Wagner Chardonnays have zero RS (i.e., no sugar).

Take another look at Appendix IV: Acids in Wine, where I explain how that sugar (RS) manages to hide acid in a wine. The highly acidic Riesling grape needs sugar to balance the natural acids.

The majority of today's wine drinkers know that the higher the RS, the sweeter the wine, but still may not understand how that sweetness—dryness—happens. Explaining Residual Sugar is a fairly easy task and one that they would may appreciate learning about in greater detail.

Made in the USA
Middletown, DE
30 December 2020